Teaching With Favorite
Newbery Books

by Lori Licciardo-Musso

SCHOLASTIC
PROFESSIONAL BOOKS

New York • Toronto • London • Auckland •
Sydney • Mexico City • New Delhi • Hong Kong

Dedication

With love to my husband, Dave, and my daughters, Brianna and

Marissa. You are truly the source of my joy, love, and inspiration.

Thank you for supporting and encouraging me.

and

In loving memory of Terry Huie, my vice-principal, my mentor, and

most of all, my friend. Our time was too short, but you will live forever

in the legacy you left behind.

Cover design by Jaime Lucero and Norma Ortiz
Cover photographs by Donnelly Marks
Interior design by Grafica Inc.
Interior photographs by Ann Musso, Leo Alvarez, and Donnelly Marks

ISBN 0-590-01975-9

Table of Contents

Out of the Dust by Karen Hesse
(1998 Newbery Medal) 6

Lily's Crossing by Patricia Reilly Giff
(1998 Newbery Honor) 9

Ella Enchanted by Gail Carson Levine
(1998 Newbery Honor) 12

The View From Saturday by E.L.
Konigsburg (1997 Newbery Medal) . . 16

A Girl Named Disaster by Nancy
Farmer (1997 Newbery Honor) 21

The Midwife's Apprentice by Karen
Cushman (1996 Newbery Medal) . . 25

Walk Two Moons by Sharon Creech
(1995 Newbery Medal) 28

The Giver by Lois Lowry
(1994 Newbery Medal) 33

Missing May by Cynthia Rylant
(1993 Newbery Medal) 36

Shiloh by Phyllis Reynolds Naylor
(1992 Newbery Medal) 39

Maniac Magee by Jerry Spinelli
(1991 Newbery Medal) 42

The True Confessions of Charlotte Doyle
by Avi (1991 Newbery Honor) 46

Number the Stars by Lois Lowry
(1990 Newbery Medal) 49

Hatchet by Gary Paulsen
(1988 Newbery Honor) 52

The Whipping Boy by Sid Fleischman
(1987 Newbery Medal) 55

Sarah, Plain and Tall by Patricia
MacLachlan (1986 Newbery Medal) . . 58

Dear Mr. Henshaw by Beverly Cleary
(1984 Newbery Medal) 61

Dicey's Song by Cynthia Voigt
(1983 Newbery Medal) 64

The Westing Game by Ellen Raskin
(1979 Newbery Medal) 67

Bridge to Terabithia by Katherine
Paterson (1978 Newbery Medal) . . . 70

The Summer of the Swans by Betsy
Byars (1971 Newbery Medal) 73

Sounder by William H. Armstrong
(1970 Newbery Medal) 77

A Wrinkle In Time by Madeleine L'Engle
(1963 Newbery Medal) 80

The Witch of Blackbird Pond by
Elizabeth George Speare (1959
Newbery Medal) 83

The Cat Who Went To Heaven by
Elizabeth Coatsworth (1931 Newbery
Medal) 86

Introduction

Each year the American Library Association awards the Newbery Medal to honor outstanding writing in children's books published in the United States. It is given to the author who has made the most distinguished contribution to children's literature during that year. This prestigious award was proposed to the American Library Association in 1921 by Frederic G. Melcher to encourage original and creative work in children's literature. Named after John Newbery, an eighteenth-century bookseller, the award was also designed to bring public recognition to quality children's literature.

The criteria for the Newbery Medal and Honor books are:

- interpretation of theme or concept
- presentation of information including accuracy, clarity, and organization
- development of plot
- delineation of characters
- delineation of setting
- appropriateness of style
- excellence of presentation for a children's audience

The committee's decision is based primarily on the text. The award is for literary quality and the quality of the presentation for children.

■ My Goals

The Newbery Medal

I love to read and always have. I can't remember a time when a book would not have been my first choice of entertainment. As a teacher, I have found great joy in passing this love of reading on to my students. My first book for Scholastic, *25 Terrific Literature Activities for Readers of All Learning Styles*, was a compilation of some of the activities I had developed to help my students become successful readers. I enjoyed writing that book and was thrilled when my editor, Virginia Dooley, called and asked if I would write a second book. You can imagine my delight when she asked if I would write one using Newbery Award books. I have read most of the Newbery Award books in preparation for this project and have found myself sailing the high seas with Charlotte Doyle (*The True Confessions of Charlotte Doyle*), caught in a tesseract (*A Wrinkle in Time*), trying to figure out a whodunit (*The Westing Game*), harboring an abused dog (*Shiloh*), and wishing with Billie Jo that she could make her mother come back to life (*Out of the Dust*)—just to mention several of the "reading journeys" I've taken.

The 25 titles I have selected to include in this book are the Newbery Award books that I felt would be used most frequently in the classroom. The choice as to what to include was difficult because all the books are such fine pieces of literature. I tried to mix the grade-level readability and present a variety of themes. I hope you will find new ideas for old favorites—and new favorites—to bring to your classroom.

■ Book Organization

The book is organized with the latest Newbery winners presented first. Each book has a short summary followed by a vocabulary list. The vocabulary list is to alert you to words that you might need to work with in your classroom. You can use your favorite vocabulary activities with these words or go over them in context.

Reading Response Journals   Each book has a list of Reading Response Journal prompts, usually presented by chapter. In my classroom, I use three-hole folders for the students' Reading Response Journals. The students keep a supply of notebook paper in the folders. They date and head the page of their journal each day with the prompt of the day and then respond to it. Students begin the next day's prompt after skipping two lines and then again heading the entry with the date and the prompt. I ask several students to share their responses at the beginning of the reading period. This opens up some great discussions on the previous night's reading and gives us a wonderful jumping-off point for the current day's reading or activity.

Chapter by Chapter   Chapter-by-chapter ideas are assignments that you can use throughout the book to help students keep track of the story as they read it. The ideas are projects rather than summaries. Designed to be fun for the students, the projects involve different learning modalities.

Into Activities   The Into activities are intended to get students excited and curious about what they are about to read, and to build their background information. Into activities should be presented prior to the reading of the book.

Through Activities   Through activities should be done during the reading of the book. These activities are used to promote comprehension and to develop critical thinking and an appreciation of language. Through activities help students navigate their way through the book.

Beyond Activities   Beyond activities are used to celebrate and evaluate a piece of literature. These activities encourage students to "go beyond," to relate events and feelings in the story to those in their own lives. Beyond activities are meant to spark continued interest in reading.

Writing Ideas   Each book contains at least one idea that can be used as a full-process-writing prompt in your Language Arts class. We know that reading and writing go hand in hand, and these ideas provide a perfect opportunity to integrate your literature and writing activities.

Out of the Dust
by Karen Hesse

1998 Newbery Winner

■ Summary

Out of the Dust is a striking work of free-verse poetry. It tells the story of 14-year-old Billie Jo's struggle and triumph after a terrible accident takes her mother's life. Scarred by the accident, Billie Jo must learn to deal with her own injuries, insecurities, and her relationship with her father amidst the cruelties of the Dust Bowl. My students could not put this book down and talked about it long after we had finished reading it.

■ Chapter by Chapter

There are twenty-four months in the book. Assign a month to each student. They will be making a class quilt that tells Billie Jo's story. Give each student a piece of 9- by 12-inch. construction paper and a white unlined sheet of 8 1/2- by 11-inch paper. After gluing the white paper in the center of the construction paper, students draw pictures to represent what happened in their months and write short descriptions of the events. When you have finished reading the book and all students have turned in their quilt pieces, ask them to put the quilt pieces together in chronological order. Don't forget to allow a piece for the title of the book. Then use a heavy needle and yarn to stitch the construction paper pieces together.

VOCABULARY

betrothal	chafed
flinch	kerosene
kin	mottled
nourish	obliged
parcel	parched
rump	sod
tart	

Hang your finished quilt in a place of honor. How about the District Office?

■ Into Ideas

Establishing Prior Knowledge Ask your students to gather as much information as they can about the Dust Bowl. Encourage them to use the Internet, the library, and family and friends as sources. I usually assign this as homework and make it like a scavenger hunt activity by asking the following question: *How much can you find out about the Dust Bowl by tomorrow?* Students bring in what they have learned and share it with the class. Then make a large chart with what your students now know about the Dust Bowl. Leave the chart up as they read the novel and add to it as students discover new things.

■ Through Ideas

Poetry   Read the first free-verse poem "Beginning: August 1920" where Billie Jo describes herself. Discuss with the students what the poem says about Billie Jo. Ask questions such as the following:

- *What aspects of Billie Jo's character do you know about now?*
- *What does the poem reveal about her?*
- *What is important to Billie Jo?*

After you have discussed Billie Jo, ask your students to write a free-verse poem about themselves. They should brainstorm the aspects of their character that it would be important for them to share with their readers. Ask your students to do self-portraits to go along with their poems—it makes a super bulletin board.

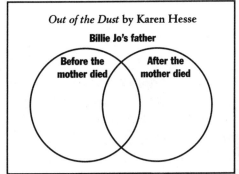

Out of the Dust by Karen Hesse

Billie Jo's father

Before the mother died / After the mother died

Venn Diagram   Divide your class into four groups and give each group one of the following Venn diagram topics: (1) Compare Billie Jo's father before and after Ma's death. (2) Compare Billie Jo's feelings about herself before and after the accident. (3) How do the townspeople treat Billie Jo before and after the accident? (4) Compare Billie Jo's life while her mother was alive with her life after her mother died. Ask each group to draw its Venn diagram on large construction paper so that it can be shared easily with the rest of the class. When a group is presenting its Venn diagram, encourage the other students to add any details that may have been overlooked.

■ Beyond Ideas

Illustrations   Ask your students to choose one of the free-verse poems in the book that really speaks to them. Discuss the following questions:

- *What kind of emotions did the poem bring out in you?*
- *Why does this particular poem stand out for you?*

After they have selected their poems, students can create illustrations to symbolize the poems. Encourage any and all kinds of artistic expression including watercolor, sketches, collages, torn paper, and so on.

Letter to Billie Jo Ask your students to write letters to Billie Jo. They can choose any time in the novel in which to correspond with her. For instance, students may choose to write condolence letters after Billie Jo's mother dies, or they may write to her at the end of the book, sharing their feelings about what she has gone through and giving advice for the future. Encourage them to take on another persona for their letters; for example, a student might pretend to be Billie Jo's father and write a letter expressing how he feels since he has been unable to express his feelings verbally to her.

■ Writing Idea

Ask students to survey family and friends about hard times in history that they have experienced, for example, the Dust Bowl, World War II, the Depression, the Vietnam War, the Civil Rights struggle, and so on. Then have each student choose one person to interview in depth. Depending on what the survey yields, you may want to put students in groups for the interviews. Each student or group can use the information from the interview to write a report or information essay about that person's place in a difficult time in history. Encourage students not only to report the facts of the incident but also to record the feelings that accompanied it.

READING RESPONSE JOURNAL PROMPTS

August 1920–January 1934: Billie Jo writes about a custom she disagrees with, losing a friend, and about two important accomplishments in her life. Choose one, and relate it to an experience in your own life.

February 1934: How does the drought influence the family's life?

March 1934: How would you describe Billie Jo's mother?

April 1934: Why does the family stay in Oklahoma if things are so bad?

May 1934: Describe something in springtime that is special to you.

June 1934: What does the harvest bring?

July 1934: Why does Billie Jo have her nightmare?

August 1934: How would you feel if you were Billie Jo?

September 1934: How have things changed since Ma died?

October/November/ December 1934: Why does everyone except Mad Dog think Billie Jo is a "poor motherless thing"? How does that make Billie Jo feel?

January 1935: What do you think Billie Jo means when she writes "Imagine" at the end of the last January 1935 entry?

February 1935: Why is playing the piano at the Palace worth the pain Billie Jo feels in her hands and arms?

March 1935: Compare Billie Jo's life to the dust storms that come and go.

April 1935: a) Why do people keep heading for California? b) Predict what Papa's spots are.

May/June 1935: Why does Billie Jo long to get out of Joyce City?

July/August 1935: What finally helps Billie Jo start to forgive her father and herself?

October 1935: How is Billie Jo's relationship with her father changing? Explain why it's changing.

November/December 1935: How has Billie Jo grown over the past year? What has caused her to grow?

Lily's Crossing
by Patricia Reilly Giff

1998 Newbery Honor Book

■ Summary

In the summer of 1944, with the advent of World War II, Lily's carefree summers at Rockaway change dramatically. Her best friend Margaret moves when her father takes a job in a wartime factory. Lily's father is sent overseas to fight in the war. Left alone with her fears, Lily finds a new friend in Albert, a young refugee from Hungary. The war has turned Albert's world upside down, too. Together, Lily and Albert rescue a kitten and begin a special friendship. They learn how secrets and lies have a way of coming back.

■ Chapter by Chapter

The chapters in *Lily's Crossing* do not have chapter titles. A fun and challenging activity for students is to think of titles for each chapter. You can foster creativity by having students share their titles with the rest of the class each day. Students are able to hear classmates' titles and get ideas about how they can improve their own. I always encourage my students to be creative and to convey the main idea of the chapter.

■ Into Ideas

World Map Give your students a blank world map, and have them find the fol-

VOCABULARY

allies	anxious
canal	censors
cicadas	convoy
D-Day	destruction
holy mackerel	hoyden
insignia	jetties
marquee	Nazi
Necco Wafers	paratroopers
patrolling	perspiration
rickety	sirens
spewing	trespassing
trestle	turrets
veering	viaduct
Walnettos	

lowing locations: New York; St. Albans; Rockaway; Germany; Detroit; Budapest; the Danube River; and Paris, France. Have students keep their maps handy as they read so that they can annotate the sites they have labeled. For example, next to Rockaway they can add "Lily's summer home" to their maps.

Guest Speaker Invite a World War II veteran and/or survivor to speak to your class. Ask them to relate to the

students what it was like here in the United States by talking about changes and challenges such as blackout curtains, food rations, women working in factories, men gone for years, and so on. Ask the speaker to help your students get a feel for the times and specifically the impact it might have had on an adolescent child.

■ Through Activities

Setting Ask your students to draw pictures of the setting of the house at Rockaway and its surrounding area. Using the novel as their guide, they should be as detailed as they can.

Letter to Poppy Lily lets her father leave for war without even saying goodbye. Have students pretend they are Lily and write letters to Poppy about why she didn't say goodbye and how she feels about him.

Lily's List Lily's problems are "lies, daydreaming, and needing friends." Tell students to list Lily's problems as they encounter the problems in the book. Also ask them to write down any resolutions that occur.

■ Beyond Ideas

Novel Newspaper Have your students produce the *Rockaway Times* newspaper. Break your class into six writing groups responsible for the following areas: lead story, feature story, editorial, arts and entertainment, advertisements, and daily living (advice, fashion, education). Remind students that they

are reporters on Rockaway Beach during the summer of 1944. They should make sure that their stories are not only significant and true to the time but also to *Lily's Crossing*. Explain to your students about the 5 W's of newspaper writing—who, what, where, why, and when. It can be helpful to bring in several samples of actual newspapers for students to refer to regarding layout and style. Many local newspapers have newspapers-in-education programs that they sponsor and are happy to send someone to speak to your students.

■ Writing Idea

Patricia Reilly Giff writes a letter to her readers at the end of *Lily's Crossing*. Read this letter with your class, and discuss the author's views on friendship. Then have your students share times that friends have made differences in their lives. Ask them to list their special friends on a piece of paper. Tell students to brainstorm events and characteristics that make that person a special friend. Based on those thoughts, have students choose one friend and write an essay letting other people know how special that person is and why he or she is such a good friend. Remind them that including specific incidents showing a person's character and attributes will make the reader more connected to this special friend. When the essays are complete, invite your students to mail the essays to their special friends.

READING RESPONSE JOURNAL PROMPTS

Chapter 1: How does Lily feel about Gram, Poppy, and her mother? How do you know?

Chapter 2: Why do you think the book *Evangeline* is so important to Lily?

Chapter 3: Why is Margaret the perfect friend for Lily?

Chapter 4: Predict what you think will happen next.

Chapter 5: Why does Lily cry?

Chapter 6: How would you feel if you were Lily at this moment?

Chapter 7: Why do you think Albert has such a strange reaction to the plane?

Chapter 8: Why doesn't Lily want to hear about Poppy or the war?

Chapter 9: Why does the mailman change his mind about giving Lily the mail instead of putting it in the mailbox?

Chapter 10: Why do you think Albert makes it so difficult to become friends with him?

Chapter 11: How is Lily feeling right now?

Chapter 12: Why do you think Albert is crying?

Chapter 13: Why does Albert doubt his parents' love for him?

Chapter 14: How can Lily get out of the lie she tells Albert, about swimming to Europe, without losing his friendship?

Chapter 15: Describe the mood in church at the special mass.

Chapter 16: What do you think the money is supposed to remind Albert of?

Chapter 17: Why is time moving so slowly for Lily?

Chapter 18: Why does Lily feel it is her fault that Albert's dreams will not come true?

Chapter 19: Why is Albert so stubborn about learning how to swim?

Chapter 20: Describe Gram's and Lily's relationship.

Chapter 21: Predict what you think Albert will say.

Chapter 22: Predict what will happen to Albert.

Chapter 23: Why would Albert take such a chance?

Chapter 24: a) According to Gram, what things do Albert's and Lily's parents do to keep them safe? b) How does Lily figure out where Poppy is?

Chapter 25: What is the real reason Lily and Albert get mad at each other?

Chapter 26: How does Lily know that Poppy has forgiven her for not saying goodbye when he left for war?

Chapter 27: Why will Rockaway never be the same for Lily and Gram?

Chapter 28: Why are Albert and Lily best friends?

Ella Enchanted
by Gail Carson Levine

1998 Newbery Honor Book

■ Summary

Ella Enchanted is a wonderful fantasy story. The fairy Lucinda gives Ella of Frell the gift of obedience. When she is with her loving family, Ella experiences no problems in being obedient. Then her mother dies, and the gift becomes a curse when Ella finds herself in the hands of people who don't care for her. In her spirited fight to free herself of the curse, Ella encounters ogres, elves, wicked stepsisters, princes, castles, giants, and fairy godmothers.

■ Chapter by Chapter

You can use the chapter title idea detailed on page 9 of this book (the **Chapter by Chapter** project for *Lily's Crossing*).

■ Into Ideas

Many mythical creatures are mentioned in this book. Before you begin reading the book, divide your class into pairs and assign a different mythical creature to each pair. Each pair should find an example of the creature in a fairy tale and then draw a picture and write a brief description of it on

unicorn

dragon

construction paper. I usually go to my local library and enlist the librarian's help. She helps me select approximately 30 different children's fairy tales to check out. I bring these fairy tales into class for students to look through to help them find their

VOCABULARY

atrocious	bestow
condescend	consumption
defiance	disdainful
docile	enamored
gullible	haughty
imitate	impertinence
inconsolable	irresistible
loathe	malice
menagerie	obedience
odious	persuade
persuasive	queue
retaliate	scruples
subterfuge	succumb
undulate	vile

creatures. Hang the finished products in the classroom. When you come to a creature in the story, the students will have their pictures and descriptions to help them visualize the situation. Here is a list of the creatures that appear in *Ella Enchanted*: hydras, dragons, unicorns, centaurs, gnomes, gryphons, fairy godmothers, elves, and ogres.

■ Through Ideas

Map of Kyrria   To help your students keep track of Ella's adventures, ask them to create maps of Kyrria that include the following locations: Frell, menagerie, Uaaxe (Giant farms), King Jerrold's castle, Jenn-Finishing School, Elves forest, and Fens (Ogres' home). Students can annotate the maps as they read the story. They can even draw Ella's route as the story unfolds.

Read Alouds   This is a great opportunity to use your read-aloud time to share classic children's fairy tales with your class. Have students chart the similarities they find in the fairy tales and discuss how the tales compare to Ella's story. A wonderful place to start is with the two fairy tales that Ella reads in her magic book, "The Shoemaker and the Elves" and "Aladdin's Lamp."

■ Beyond Ideas

Create A Mythical Country   Ask your students to create their own mythical countries. They should begin by picking real-world locations for their countries. They can place the countries in the middle of a continent or out in the ocean. I ask each student to give me the longitude and latitude of the new country. Then they must research the climates and terrain of those locations and use the information in creating their new countries. From that point on, students can be as creative as they like. I ask them to brainstorm their favorite things to use as possible themes for their mythical countries. For example, let's say someone loves chocolate. That student might call his or her new country Chocolate Kiss Island. Then students create the rest of

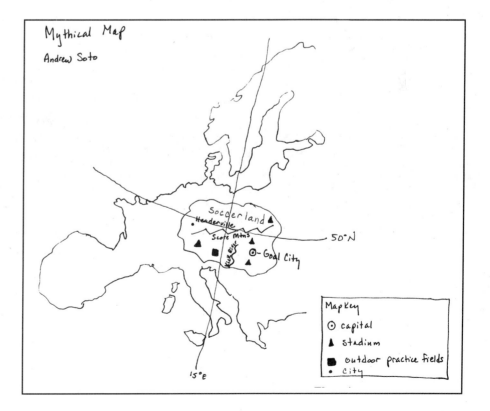

the country using their theme and incorporating the following items: rivers, lakes, mountains, deserts, oceans, cities, a capital, and so on. I have them look at a lot of maps to get ideas. My students then draw their own maps of their mythical countries. I grade them by how accurate the climate and geographical features are to their longitude and latitude, how well the themes run throughout their maps, and their attention to detail.

Other Versions of Cinderella Since *Ella Enchanted* turns out to be a twist on the Cinderella story, suggest that your students check out other versions of this classic story. There are many different versions from different countries. I place my students in groups of four and ask them to select one of the different versions of Cinderella. The group reads and charts the story, showing the characters, the plot, the conflict, and the resolution. The groups share their charts with the rest of the class, and we discuss the similarities and differences among the stories. Versions include *Yeh-Shen* retold by Ai-Ling Louie (Chinese); *The Rough-Faced Girl* by Rafe Martin (Algonquin); *Sootface* retold by Robert D. San Souci (Ojibwa); *Jouanah* adapted by Jewell Reinhart Coburn with Tzexa Cherta Lee (Hmong); *The Egyptian Cinderella* by Shirley Climo; *The Korean Cinderella* by Shirley Climo; *The Starlight Cloak* retold by Jenny Nimmo (Celtic); *The Turkey Girl* retold by Penny Pollock (Zuni); *The Philippine Cinderella* by Myrna J. de la Paz; *Kongi and Potgi* adapted by Oki S. Han and Stephanie

Haboush Plunkett (Korean); *Ashpet* retold by Joanne Compton (Appalachian); *The Golden Sandal* by Rebecca Hickox (Middle Eastern); *Cendrillon* by Robert D. San Souci (Caribbean); and *Cinder-Elly* by Frances Minters (modern).

■ Writing Idea

Throughout this novel, your students have a lot of exposure to fairy tales. Your Into activity introduced them to different creatures in fairy tales. Your Through activities showed students different parts of a kingdom and exposed them to classic fairy tales, and your Beyond activities helped them with vocabulary and the different twists that fairy tales can take. Now is a perfect time to let your students be creative and write their own fairy tales. Remind them of the characteristics that all fairy tales have in common and brainstorm some ideas with them. A fun thing to do with the completed fairy tales is to make them into big books to share with elementary school buddies. I have always found kindergarten and first grade teachers very willing to have older students come in and share their stories with the younger children. It can be a great experience for both classes and really gives your students a reason to be particularly careful and clever when writing their fairy tales.

READING RESPONSE JOURNAL PROMPTS

Chapter 1: Why does Lucinda's gift turn out to be a curse?

Chapter 2: Explain Ella's feelings.

Chapter 3: Why isn't Ella close to her father?

Chapter 4: Why is the thought of finishing school frightening to Ella?

Chapter 5: How does Mandy try to comfort Ella?

Chapter 6: Why are the ogres so dangerous? How can Ella break the curse without hurting the little gnome and herself?

Chapter 7: Why is it important that people not know about Ella's curse?

Chapter 8: Why is Hattie so mean to Ella?

Chapter 9: How does Ella feel about finishing school now?

Chapter 10: Why isn't Ella pleased with her progress at school?

Chapter 11: Why is Areida so important to Ella?

Chapter 12: Why do you think the three letters appeared in Ella's magic book?

Chapter 13: Why are the elves helpful to Ella?

Chapter 14: Why don't the ogres eat Ella?

Chapter 15: How does Ella help the prince?

Chapter 16: Why is Ella's heart beating so fast?

Chapter 17: Why are the other fairies mad at Lucinda?

Chapter 18: Do you think Lucinda's new command is better than the old one? Explain why or why not.

Chapter 19: What is your opinion of Ella's father?

Chapter 20: Explain whether you think Lucinda's latest gift is a blessing or a curse. What could be the implications of this gift?

Chapter 21: How do you think Ella will pay for having fun with Char?

Chapter 22: Predict what Ella's stepfamily might do.

Chapter 23: Why does Ella have to turn to her father for help?

Chapter 24: How will Ella respond to Char?

Chapter 25: What do you think will happen next?

Chapter 26: Why do you think Mandy is worried about Ella using Lucinda to help her get to the ball?

Chapter 27: Why is the Prince drawn to Lela?

Chapter 28: Describe Ella's feelings at the moment Hattie pulls off her mask. Describe Prince Charmont's feelings.

Chapter 29: Why was Ella finally able to break the curse?

Chapter 30: Do you think they will truly live happily ever after? Tell why or why not.

The View From Saturday

by E. L. Konigsburg

1997 Newbery Medal

▪ Summary

Mrs. Olinski puts four students together to form an Academic Bowl team. The four students—Noah, Nadia, Ethan, and Julian—are an unlikely group. They come from very different backgrounds and have different interests, yet they begin a strong friendship. The team proves to be unbeatable in the Academic Bowl, and in life. This is a great story about appreciating and enjoying people's differences.

▪ Chapter by Chapter

I asked my students to do a story trail for this book and got some really creative results. The simplest way to do a story trail is to have students create a picture and short summary for each chapter. They do this all on one piece of large construction paper in a maze-like format. Along the way, they add details to their trails that represent the story line. The fun and real learning begins when students get creative with their work. They can show peaks and valleys relating to the action in the chapter. The story trail can become a metaphor for the whole novel. It really helps students keep track of what's going on as the story unfolds.

VOCABULARY

acronyms	incarnation
laxatives	Mazel tov
paraplegic	podium
reincarnation	ruggelach
tranquilizers	

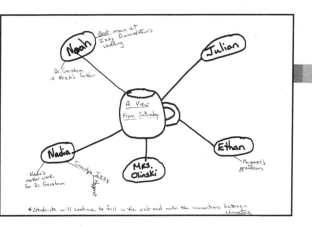

■ Into Ideas

Title Impression The title *The View From Saturday* is an interesting one. I asked my students to tell me in writing what they thought a story with this title might be about. The responses covered a wide range. Everyone shared their responses, and then I kept them so that we could revisit them at the end of the novel. Prior to reading the novel, students hypothesized that the story was about a town named Saturday, or a look back from a long hard week, and so on. When I handed the papers back at the end of the novel, the discussion became very lively. None of my students agreed with their first impressions of the story title, but interestingly enough, there were still many differences of opinion as to why the author chose this title. Students suggested that Saturday was the end of all the Souls' journeys; things always look different and better on Saturdays; the story was about appreciating differences; and Saturday is a day of the week when you have fewer commitments, so you could try different things; or simply that Saturday was the day they won the contest and was their tea day. The discussion really made my class think.

■ Through Ideas

Character Webs Not only does *The View From Saturday* have many characters to remember, it is also a challenge to keep track of their many and different relationships. A character web is an excellent activity for this book. Students put the title of the book in the center of their papers, circle it, and draw lines out from the circle as each character appears. Each character's name should be accompanied by his or her characteristics as well as a description of his or her role in the story. If characters make a connection, such as that Mrs. Olinski's first principal was Margaret Draper, then a dotted line should be drawn between the two characters and the nature of the connection should be written on the line.

Scrapbooks A fun and challenging activity for students is to ask them to create a scrapbook for one of the four main characters—Noah, Nadia, Ethan, or Julian. I brought in some samples of scrapbooks for

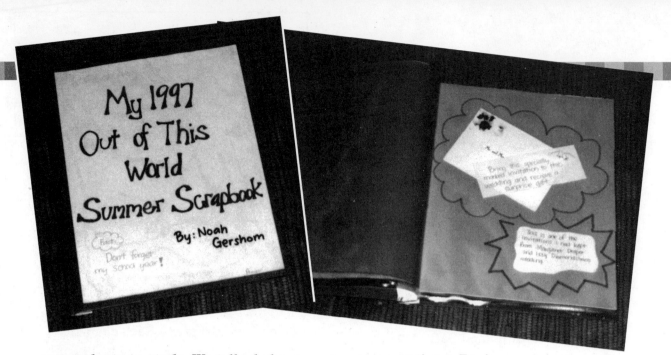

my students to study. We talked about how they differ from photo albums in that people place items in them like ticket stubs, a restaurant menu, confetti from a cruise ship, a theater program, a napkin from a wedding, and so on. I then require the students to place at least ten items in each character's scrapbook. Each item must have a brief explanation as to what it is and how it fits in the story.

Drama   My students have a great time reenacting short scenes from *The View From Saturday*. I allow them to find places in the book that they think would be fun to act out. They can work in pairs or groups of four or however many students are needed to act out the scene. Students write the page numbers of their scenes on the board, and then no one else in the class can choose those scenes. This insures that the class will get to see many parts of the book acted out. The students have one class period to work on their scenes. They are not required to have costumes or props. I arrange the groups in chronological order for their presentations. Each day, two or three groups present their scenes until we have seen all the groups perform. Some scenes that you might want to consider are Nadia and Ethan, pp. 44–47; Noah and Nadia, pp. 82–83; the Souls, pp. 90–91; or the Souls (Annie), pp. 99–101.

■ Beyond Ideas

Journey Illustrations   In the book, Mrs. Olinski talks about the separate journeys that each character has taken, and she herself has taken a journey. I break my class into five groups and assign to each group one of the following characters: Nadia, Noah, Julian, Ethan, or Mrs. Olinski. Each group is responsible for making a visual map of that character's journey. Here are some questions for groups to consider:

- *Where does each character start?*
- *What are the triumphs, hurts, and ups and downs along the way?*

Every part of the character's journey should be annotated so that it is easily understood.

Tea Party Tea time is crucial to the Souls. For this activity, I collect as many tea sets as I can for my classroom. I share with my students the history of tea time, and then we talk about how it was used in the novel. I then put my students at tables of four; each table has a tea set. They then serve the tea and discuss the novel. It's a fun twist for the students—and a very civilized time! I ask my students to talk about each character individually first, focusing on questions such as these:

- *How did that character change during the novel?*
- *What characteristics made that character special?*
- *Why did Mrs. Olinski pick that particular character to be on the Academic Bowl team?*

After they have discussed the four main characters individually, I ask them to talk about what made them into the Souls. How did the character's uniqueness make her or him a perfect fit for the group? What did you learn from this book?

■ Writing Idea

Have students write essays on discrimination. Begin by encouraging them to think about the novel *The View From Saturday* by posing the following questions:

- *How was each of the characters discriminated against?*
- *Did they ever discriminate against anyone else?*
- *What are the results of discrimination? Can it be overcome? If so, how can it be overcome?*

- *How can small incidents of discrimination tear down or build up our world?*
- *What solutions can you offer?*

I tell students to write their essays using specific incidents of discrimination either from the book or from their own lives. I ask them to express how each incident affected the person discriminated against and the people around them, and how the person handled it.

READING RESPONSE JOURNAL PROMPTS

Chapter 1: Predict what will happen next.
"Noah Writes...Letter": a) What does Tillie mean when she says the ballpoint pen is the biggest single factor in the decline of Western Civilization? How does that compare to Mother's remark about the decline of Western Civilization? b) Why does Noah start his B & B letter saying thank you for a vacation that was out of this world? What does he mean?

Chapter 2: What is your impression of Dr. Roy Clayton Rohmer?
"Nadia tells of Turtle Love": a) How has Nadia's life changed in the last year physically and emotionally? b) Why does Nadia think "Inside me there was a lot of best friendship that no one but Ginger was using."?

Chapter 3: Explain the difference between sixth graders who ask "Now what?" and sixth graders who ask "So what?".
"Ethan Explains...Inn": a) How does Ethan feel about his brother Luke? How does the community feel about Luke and Ethan? b) Using a Venn diagram, compare and contrast farmers and suburbanites. c) How can silence be a habit that hurts? How would you have reacted to the book bag incident if you were Julian? How do you think he felt? What do you think of the message Julian wrote on his book bag? d) If you could live one day of your life all over again, what day would it be? Explain your choice.

Chapter 4: Why do the Souls want to help Mrs. Olinski?
"Julian Narrates...Sandy": How does Julian finally get even with Ham Knapp?

Chapter 5: Why is Mrs. Olinski jealous of Margaret and Izzy?

Chapter 6: Why are the Souls such a great Academic Bowl team?

Chapter 7: a) Why is Dr. Rohmer so worried about Mr. Fairbain? b) What is the significance of the sixth celebration?

Chapter 8: What is the difference between incarnation and reincarnation?

Chapter 9: How does the community get involved in the state championship?

Chapter 10: What does Mrs. Olinski mean when she says Julian makes each mile a journey of quarter inches?

Chapter 11: What does "if you've not seen something, it's hard to know what is missing" mean?

A Girl Named Disaster
by Nancy Farmer

1997 Newbery Honor Book

■ Summary

A Girl Named Disaster centers around a young African woman named Nhamo. She is on a perilous journey to find her father and escape from an impending marriage to a cruel man. The journey would be hard for anyone, let alone a young girl of eleven. Nhamo must deal with near drowning, starvation, and loneliness. She learns to be resourceful, and she finds strength from the teaching of her ancestors.

■ Chapter by Chapter

This is a very long, sophisticated, and sometimes complicated book. I really feel that I need to guide my students through it, so we read most of the book aloud in class. For the chapter by chapter idea, I have each of my students randomly pull a number from a box of numbers I have prepared (1–42 for the number of chapters). Everyone writes a summary for the chapter number he or she draws. Since I have 32 students in my class, I always ask if anyone would like to draw an extra number and receive credit for the additional summary. I check the summaries for accuracy, mechanics, and spelling and then run off copies for each student in the class. Students keep these summaries in their reading response journals.

VOCABULARY

A detailed vocabulary list is given at the end of *A Girl Named Disaster*.

■ Into Ideas

Animal Mini-Reports   Many unusual animals are part of *A Girl Named Disaster*. Before I begin the book with my class, I assign an animal mini-report to pairs of students. A mini-report consists of a picture of the animal and a one-page description of the animal–where it lives, what its habits are, and so on. Partners share their reports with the class and then add it to our *A Girl Named Disaster* bulletin board. This way, as the animals come up in the story, students can check the board to remind them of what that the animal looks like and what its characteristics are. Animals that I use include jackals, bush pigs, honey badgers, porcupines, hippos, warthogs, elephants, crocodiles, black scorpions, baboons, cane rats, kudus, antelope, anteaters, mongooses, dassies, caracals, and servals.

Venn Diagrams   This story shows a young girl struggling with a clash of cultures and religions. I ask my stu-

dents to do some research into Christianity and the Shona religion. To focus their research, I pose questions such as the following:

- *What do the two religions have in common?*
- *How are they different?*
- *What are the beliefs of each religion?*

This way, when students come to the struggle in the book, they will have some background knowledge.

■ Through Ideas

Setting Dioramas There are six main settings in *A Girl Named Disaster*. I split my class into six groups. I usually let the class decide on these groups because they will need to do some

work outside school for this activity. Each group randomly selects a setting—the Village, the Trading Post, Garden Island, Efifi, Jongwe's home, and Father's grave site. As the setting comes up in the book, that particular group works on re-creating the setting in a shoe box diorama. We leave the dioramas on display until we are finished with the novel.

Storytelling There are some marvelous stories told within the story of Nhamo—stories that teach lessons. I ask my students to work in groups of three or four to create an illustrated children's book using one of the stories. They retell the story in their own words and give the moral at the end. Book construction can be as simple as stapling sheets of plain paper inside a construction-paper cover. Since many students have had bookmaking experience, they may enjoy making more sophisticated books. Some of the stories in *A Girl Named Disaster* that would work are Mother Earth, pp. 95–97; *njuzu*, pp. 113–115; baboon totem, pp. 148–150; one daughter, pp. 161–163; Princess Senwa, pp. 175–178; Farmer and baboons, pp. 203–204; Three Kings, pp. 243–244; only one son, pp. 249–250; and hyena and jackal, pp. 277–278.

■ Beyond Ideas

Personal Totems Ask your students to research African totem poles, particularly the significance of the animals used in the totems and the importance of their order. Suggest that they take a look at some pictures of ancient totem poles. Encourage students to create totem poles to represent their families. I have my students draw their totem poles and write brief descriptions of their meanings.

Coming of Age Poster   I ask my students to find several parts of the novel where Nhamo's character changed and grew. They create posters that show Nhamo's coming of age. Each poster should have three parts: (1) where Nhamo started, (2) events that caused Nhamo to grow and progress towards maturity, and (3) her final coming of age. Students

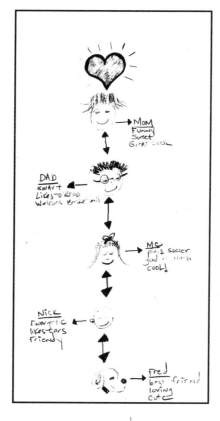

copy passages from the book to fit each category and then describe why they chose each passage. Each section of the poster should contain an illustration. The result is a visual representation of Nhamo's growth as a character.

■ Writing Idea

Present this writing idea to students: You have been asked to write a biography on Nhamo to be included in a book about famous women of Africa. Your editor has limited you to one typed page. Remember, you want your readers to be moved by Nhamo's triumphs and trials and to gain a sense of how great her accomplishments were.

READING RESPONSE JOURNAL PROMPTS

Chapter 1: a) According to Ambuya, why do her people have to work hard and have lives full of strife and danger? b) Why do you think Aunt Chipo is so easy on Masvita?

Chapter 2: a) Why is Nhamo afraid of leopards? b) Why doesn't Nhamo go directly back to Aunt Chipo after she collects firewood?

Chapter 3: a) According to Uncle Kufa, what happens to children who don't obey their parents? b)

Why is Nhamo so worried about a person's spirit? How do you think Nhamo feels about her father? c) Why doesn't Ambuya comfort Nhamo after Masvita leaves?

Chapter 4: Why was *roora* so important? What does it say about this culture's view of women?

Chapter 5: What do you think will happen next after Uncle Kufa finds leopard tracks on Vatete's grave?

Chapter 6: How does fear affect the village?

Chapter 7: a) Why does Nhamo think her family and the other villagers are afraid of her? b) Compare and contrast the setting of the village with the setting of the trading post.

Chapter 8: a) Nhamo means "disaster." Why is she called Nhamo? b) Why are Uncle Kufu and Aunt Chipo worried that

READING RESPONSE JOURNAL PROMPTS (CONTINUED)

Ambuya has told the story of Nhamo's father to strangers? c) How does the author support the meanings of Nhamo's and Masvita's names in the book?

Chapter 9: How would you feel after visiting Muvuki if you were Nhamo?

Chapter 10: Why is it important for Jo to let Muvuki maintain his supremacy even if it were to mean losing Nhamo?

Chapter 11: What are the pros and cons of Nhamo's two choices—marriage to Zororo Mtoko or running away to the Catholics?

Chapter 12: Why is it important for Ambuya to tell Nhamo that Muvuki is wrong and that Aunt Chipo is lying?

Chapter 13: What is the difference between an illness of the body and an illness of the spirit?

Chapter 14: How does Nhamo change in this chapter?

Chapter 15: What is the significance of Nhamo's dream?

Chapter 16: Why is Nhamo getting discouraged?

Chapter 17: Explain the following phrase: "the paths of the body are long but the paths of the spirit are weak."

Chapter 18: How do you think

Nhamo's dream about Long Teats will affect her?

Chapter 19: Why does Nhamo leave the island?

Chapter 20: Nhamo changes dramatically from the beginning of this chapter to the end. Why does he?

Chapter 21: a) How does Nhamo ease her loneliness? b) What is Nhamo thinking about the baboon?

Chapter 22: Why does Nhamo have mixed emotions about her victory over the baboons?

Chapter 23: Summarize Nhamo's plan for survival.

Chapter 24: Compare Uncle Kufa and his friends to the baboons.

Chapter 25: What is happening to Nhamo?

Chapter 26: Why does Nhamo cry when she kills the dassie?

Chapter 27: Why does Nhamo react so strangely to Tag's grooming her?

Chapter 28: What emotions does Nhamo experience in this chapter?

Chapter 29: What do you think the significance of the burning of Nhamo's mother's picture will be?

Chapter 30: What is the terrible wailing shriek Nhamo hears? What causes it?

Chapter 31: Why is Nhamo more fearful of the new dangers?

Chapter 32: Where do you think Nhamo is?

Chapter 33: Describe Nhamo's new setting.

Chapter 34: Why does Nhamo find it hard to leave Efifi and search for her father?

Chapter 35: a) Why does Nhamo start referring to Mother as Dr. Masuku? b) Why is Baba Joseph uncomfortable with Nhamo's story?

Chapter 36: Predict what will happen next.

Chapter 37: What happens that night on Karoyi Mountain?

Chapter 38: Why does Nhamo cry out "Ambuya"?

Chapter 39: Why do the Jongwes accept Nhamo into their family?

Chapter 40: What happens to Nhamo's *roora*?

Chapter 41: Why do Nhamo's feelings about leopards change?

Chapter 42: How has Nhamo joined her new life to her old life?

The Midwife's Apprentice
by Karen Cushman

1996 Newbery Medal

■ Summary

In fourteenth-century medieval England, a young homeless girl known as Brat finds shelter in a farmer's dung heap. The village midwife, Jane, finds Brat and takes her as an apprentice. Jane gives Brat a new name, Beetle, and works her very hard. Beetle learns the skills of a midwife, gains a friend, and adopts a cat. Beetle rechristens herself Alyce. As Alyce, she fights to overcome her failures and find the good inside herself.

■ Chapter by Chapter

Little books are fun for students to make. The books also help them keep track of the action as it unfolds in each chapter. I ask students to fold plain 8 1/2- by 11-inch paper in half vertically and cut the paper along the fold. Then they fold half-sheet vertically until they have enough for a title page and a page for each chapter. For this book, students need 8 half-sheets of paper to make a 16-page books. Tell them to fold and staple construction-paper covers to the outside of the books. Students design and illustrate their covers and title pages, and on each subsequent page, they draw a picture and write a summary for each chapter as they read it.

VOCABULARY

bailiff	blight
clodpole	comfrey
compendium	curdled
dawdle	dire
dung	exertions
flax	heedless
ignorance	meandered
paternosters	pluck
reluctant	resistance
revelers	scrawny
solemnity	soothsayers
stanching	surfeit
tantalizing	taunted
tormented	treachery
unnourished	whiffler
wimple	

■ Into Ideas

Author's Note   Read the author's note at the back of the novel. The note discusses medieval England, midwifery, herbal knowledge, and the superstitions of the time. I read this with my students and discuss why they think certain things worked, why midwifery

disappeared for a while, and why midwifery has become so popular again. This gives students some background knowledge that helps them understand Jane and Alyce.

Guest Speaker   Students are fascinated to hear an actual practitioner talk about her or his profession. Inviting a midwife to speak to your class is the best way to inform students about the profession. When you invite a midwife to speak, make sure to do the following: (1) invite a licensed midwife, (2) get parental permission for each student, and (3) talk to the midwife to set up the direction of the talk prior to the visit. I ask the midwife to talk about her job, the history of the profession, and its importance and popularity but to stay away from graphic birth descriptions and not to show any videos.

■ Through Ideas

Character Trait Posters   The characters in *The Midwife's Apprentice* are unusual and colorful. A character trait poster is a fun activity that helps students really take a look at the characters. Ask students to pick a main character such as Alyce, Jane, Will, or Jennet and draw a picture of the character at the center of a large piece of drawing paper. Around the character's picture, they can write direct quotes from the novel that describe that character's traits. I have them supply two quotes for each of these categories: personality, wants/desires/ambitions, relationship with other characters, speech as it relates to aspects of

his/her personality, and appearance. Students should label their categories or use symbols to designate categories. At the bottom of the posters, they write original paragraphs analyzing their characters.

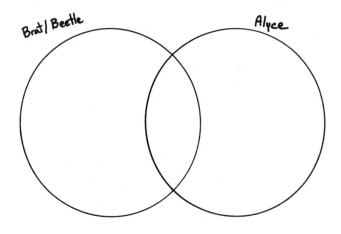

Venn Diagram   Ask students to look at the changes in the main character by creating a Venn diagram comparing and contrasting Brat/Beetle to Alyce.

■ Beyond Ideas

Continuing the Story   *The Midwife's Apprentice* ends with Alyce asserting herself and returning to be Jane Sharp's apprentice. It is always a rewarding challenge to ask students to write the next chapter in a book that ends in this fashion. My students always ask, "What happened to Alyce?", "How does Jane treat her?" and so on. This is a perfect opportunity to let students show you how they think this story should have ended.

■ Writing Idea

Give students an opportunity to become apprentices in occupations of their choice. Although they can't actually apprentice themselves, they may be able to spend the day on the job with someone or, at the very least, interview someone who has a job in which they are interested. Prior to giving this assignment, I survey the parents in my classroom. I ask if they would be willing to help students find out about their professions and if they know of anyone else who might be willing to help out. I compile a list of these volunteers and their occupations to share with students. I encourage students to gain firsthand experience with the job or to interview someone on the list. Before I send my students out, we rehearse proper interview questions and demeanor. I always have to remind students that asking their mentors exactly how much money they make could be considered rude. I ask students to write reports or informational essays on the occupations to share with the class.

Adrienne Rozier

An architect

Architects design buildings. They come up with building plans that construction workers follow. They have to plan everything like where the walls will go, where the windows should go, and where pipes and wires should go.

Architects have to go to college for at least four years. Then they take a test so they can get a license to be an architect.

Architects want to be sure buildings work right. But they also want buildings to look good. That's why it's a good idea to have an architect design all new buildings.

READING RESPONSE JOURNAL PROMPTS

Chapter 1: What do the names Brat, Beetle, and the Midwife's Apprentice tell you about this girl?

Chapter 2: What does Beetle's interaction with the cat tell you about her past?

Chapter 3: Why doesn't Jane Sharp want Beetle to learn her midwife's skills?

Chapter 4: Why does Beetle stay when she is treated so poorly by everyone?

Chapter 5: Why does Beetle take on the name Alyce?

Chapter 6: Why does Will finally call Beetle Alyce?

Chapter 7: What leads the villagers to believe that the Devil has come to their village?

Chapter 8: Why does the birth of the calves cause Alyce to learn about singing and songs?

Chapter 9: Why does Alyce finally smile?

Chapter 10: How has Alyce changed since the beginning of the novel?

Chapter 11: Why can't Alyce cry?

Chapter 12: Why does Magister Reese teach the cat to read?

Chapter 13: Why is Alyce a failure?

Chapter 14: What brings Alyce back to the village?

Chapter 15: What point is the author trying to make when Alyce asks "was she even pretty under the dirt?"

Chapter 16: Why does Alyce finally laugh?

Chapter 17: Why does Jane Sharp let Alyce return as her apprentice?

1995 Newbery Medal

Walk Two Moons
by Sharon Creech

■ Summary

Walk Two Moons is two stories woven into one. Salamanca Tree Hiddle tells her grandparents about her friend Phoebe Winterbottom. As Sal tells Phoebe's story—a story that is sometimes funny but deeply emotional—her own story is revealed. Both girls experience the loss of their mothers—one permanently, the other temporarily—and must come to terms with the loss and the changes it brings.

■ Chapter by Chapter

This story unfolds so quickly and is so engaging that your students will want to move through it quickly. There are 44 chapters in the book, and if students have to stop at each chapter to do an activity, they may resent it.

VOCABULARY

anonymous	besieging
caboodle	cantankerous
chaotic	damsel
defiance	devour
diabolic	distress
elaborated	gallantly
gullible	lunatic
malevolent	omnipotent
ornery	pandemonium
parched	peculiar
shrapnel	

Here's an idea that will help them process each chapter without being tedious. Ask students to make a symbolic pizza of *Walk Two Moons*. First they cut out a large tag board circle. The circle should be at least 8 inches in diameter. On one side of the tag board, have students make a collage from pictures cut out of magazines. The collage should represent the themes and events in *Walk Two Moons*. Be sure to have students leave room along the edge (crust) to write the title of the book and their own names. Have them divide their circles into 6 equal parts. Each slice of the pizza will contain a summary of seven chapters; for example, one slice for chapters 1–7; one slice for chapters 8–14, one slice for chapters 15–21, and so on. Stopping after every seventh chapter for a review is not too tedious and provokes deeper thought about the text.

■ Into Ideas

Map of the United States In this novel, Sal and her grandparents take a long trip across the United States. To help students prepare for the novel, I give them outline maps of the United States and ask them to label the places:

Bybanks, Kentucky	Ohio River
Euclid, Ohio	Lewiston, Idaho
Washington, D.C.	Philadelphia
South Bend, Indiana	Illinois
Lake Michigan	Chicago, Illinois
Madison, Wisconsin	Pipestone, Minnesota
Sioux Falls, South Dakota	Lake Mendota
Lake Monona	Rocky Mountains
Wyoming	Montana
Mitchell, South Dakota	Chamberlain, South Dakota
Badlands, South Dakota	Missouri River
Mount Rushmore	Yellowstone Park

Students can use these maps to trace the route that Sal and her grandparents took on their journey.

Travel Brochures Ask students to create travel brochures highlighting some of the places that Sal and her grandparents visit. Travel brochures can easily be created by folding an 8 1/2- by 11-inch piece of paper into three equal parts. Students can use photos or magazine pictures to represent the sites at each attraction and write a catchy paragraph that would entice people to want to visit the place. I bring in several brochures from travel agencies to give students some ideas as to content and layout. Another great way to do this is to use the computer program Microsoft Publisher to make your brochures. The computer program is easy to use, and it makes the brochures look very professional. When students arrive at each destination in the book, they will be reminded of what each site has to offer and will have a better picture of what's going on.

■ Through Ideas

Murals Five mysterious messages are left for the Winterbottoms.

1. Don't judge a man until you've walked two moons in his moccasins.
2. Everyone has his own agenda.
3. In the course of a lifetime, what does it matter?
4. You can't keep the birds of sadness from flying over your head, but you can keep them from nesting in your hair.
5. We never know the worth of water until the well is dry.

I divide my class into five groups and give each group one of the messages.

Each group is to interpret the meaning of its message in a mural. The mural must include the message and symbols or pictures that convey its meaning. Students can also write what they think the message means or paraphrase it to go along with the pictures.

Drawings of the Soul   In the book, the students in Sal's class are asked to draw their souls. The results are profound and say a lot about the students. After my students have read that part of the book (page 129), I ask them to draw their own souls. We follow the same procedure as the book does by displaying the pictures without names and trying to figure out which picture belongs to which person.

Venn Diagrams   Have students make Venn diagrams comparing Mrs. Winterbottom's departure to Sugar's leaving. They can also do Venn diagrams comparing Phoebe's response to her mother's leaving with Sal's response to her mother's departure. Another idea is to compare the Hiddles to the Pickfords or to compare the Winterbottoms to Sal's family. All of these make for interesting discussions.

Poems   Have on hand the poems mentioned in the novel—the e.e. cummings poem "the little

horse is newly" and Longfellow's poem "The Tide Rises, The Tide Falls." Discuss students' responses to the poems.

■ Beyond Ideas

What's in a Name?   The meaning of names is very important in Sal's family. It is always fun to ask your students to find out the meaning of their own names and any stories that go along with them. Many parents have beautiful or funny stories to share with their children about what their names mean and how the names were chosen. I also have on hand several books about the meanings and roots of names for students to examine. I give students the opportunity to make fancy nameplates for themselves that include the meanings of their names

Personal Journals I ask students to keep their own personal journals so that they can have records of their personal journeys in life. They can bring in their own journals, or I provide them with composition books to be used as journals. Since these journals are private, I don't read them. I do, however, provide students with one period of sustained silent writing time once a week to work on journals (for my class, it's every Friday for 15 minutes). At the end of that time, I simply walk around the room and check to see that students have written in their journals. I encourage them to write about the trials and triumphs of the past week. I also suggest that they follow Oprah's advice and write about what they are grateful for in the past week. My students look forward to this time. I store the journals, but students are free to take them home to work on as long as they bring them to class each Friday.

■ Writing Idea

Walk Two Moons is about the importance of family and friends, and there is a special emphasis placed on mothers. This is a nice time to ask your students to write about what their own mothers mean to them. Have them mail their finished work to their mothers. You'll get a lot of positive feedback from moms. I am always concerned when I give an assignment like this because I do have students who have lost their mothers or find it difficult to write about them, so I give the option of writing an essay about grandparents or a best friend. Both of these characters were important in the novel also.

READING RESPONSE JOURNAL PROMPTS

Chapter 1: How do you think Sal feels right now?

Chapter 2: Compare your grandparents to the Hiddles.

Chapter 3: Do you think Sal is brave? Explain your reasons.

Chapter 4: Why doesn't Sal want to like Margaret?

Chapter 5: How would you feel if you were Sal watching Gramps help the "damsel in distress"?

Chapter 6: Compare Phoebe's home life to Sal's.

Chapter 7: Why do you think Sal keeps hearing the whispers "rush, hurry, rush"?

Chapter 8: Why do you think the young man wants to see Mrs. Winterbottom?

Chapter 9: Predict who the message is for and why it was sent.

Chapter 10: Why doesn't Sal want to send postcards to anyone?

Chapter 11: Why does Sal flinch when other people touch her?

Chapter 12: Why is Gramps's bed so important to him?

Chapter 13: Predict what kind of trouble the journals will cause.

Chapter 14: Compare Sal's feelings towards her father to Phoebe's feelings towards her mother.

Chapter 15: Discuss how the boy changes in this chapter.

Chapter 16: Why do you think the whispers are starting to say "slow down"?

Chapter 17: a) What's wrong with Mrs. Winterbottom? b) Why does Sal seem to see Mrs. Winterbottom's discontent when her two daughters don't notice?

Chapter 18: Why do Sal and her father have to leave Euclid?

Chapter 19: What do you think Phoebe's "lunatic" wants?

Chapter 20: What is going through Sal's mind when she finds out Phoebe's mother has gone away?

Chapter 21: Why do you think Sal's and Ben's images of their souls are the same?

Chapter 22: a) Why are "fishes in the air" helpful to Sal and Phoebe as they deal with their mothers' leaving? b) What does Sal's father mean when he says "A person isn't a bird. You can't cage a person."?

Chapter 23: Why is Sal afraid of pregnant women?

Chapter 24: What does the latest message mean to you?

Chapter 25: Do you think Mr. Winterbottom was crying? Explain your opinion.

Chapter 26: Why is Phoebe driving Sal crazy?

Chapter 27: How does helping Phoebe deal with her mother's disappearance help Sal?

Chapter 28: Why is Sal afraid of things that she had never been afraid of before her mother left?

Chapter 29: How would you feel if you were Mr. Winterbottom?

Chapter 30: Why does Sal decide she needs to find Mrs. Winterbottom?

Chapter 31: Predict what will happen next.

Chapter 32: How would you feel if part of your journal were read aloud in class?

Chapter 33: Why does Sal start to think of Mrs. Cadaver in a different light?

Chapter 34: Why is Gram so touched by Old Faithful?

Chapter 35: What do you think is going to happen tomorrow?

Chapter 36: How will Phoebe react?

Chapter 37: What attracts Sal and Ben to each other?

Chapter 38: Write what you think each individual Winterbottom is thinking tonight.

Chapter 39: What is each Winterbottom feeling right now?

Chapter 40: What's wrong with Gram?

Chapter 41: How would you feel in Sal's place?

Chapter 42: Why does Sal finally accept the fact that her mother isn't coming back?

Chapter 43: How do you feel right now?

Chapter 44: Why are the Hiddles able to go back to Bybanks?

The Giver
by Lois Lowry

1994 Newbery Medal

■ Summary

The Giver shows what life might be like in a community where there was no pain or inconvenience of any kind. In this community, everyone follows the rules and rituals and is well cared for. At the age of twelve, each resident receives a job that is perfectly suited to her or him. When Jonas turns twelve, he is given the high honor of becoming the new Receiver. The Receiver is the only person who holds memories for the community. Tied to those memories are overwhelming feelings that make Jonas question the community in which he was raised.

VOCABULARY

admonition	anguish
apprehensive	aptitude
assuage	benign
chastise	excruciating
intrigued	isolation
lethargy	palpable
permeated	petulantly
resignation	vigilant

■ Chapter by Chapter

Instead of doing a chapter by chapter project for this novel, I have my students make a step book so they can analyze the tools that the author uses. To make a step book, students will need four sheets of paper. They stack the four sheets on top of each other but staggered at the top by half an inch each. Then they hold the staggered sheets in their left hands and, with their right hands, reach underneath and fold the sheets up to half an inch below the fourth stagger. This will result in a book with seven graduated steps. The top page is for the title of the novel, an illustration,

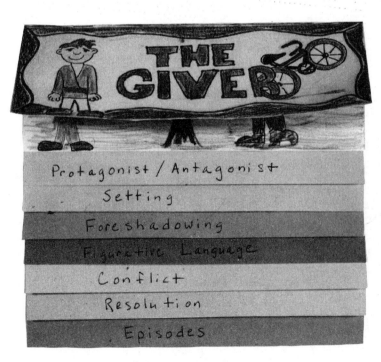

and the student's name. The seven steps should be labeled as follows: Protagonist/Antagonist, Setting, Foreshadowing, Figurative Language, Conflict, Resolution, and Episodes. The students open each page to reveal space for them to illustrate the meaning of each step and to write what it means. For the Episodes step, students should pick one scene from the beginning of the book, two scenes from the middle, and an ending scene to give the overall idea of the novel.

▪ Into Ideas

A Perfect World   Ask students to write what their ideas of a perfect world would be. Have them consider the following questions:

- *How would you create this perfect world?*
- *What kinds of rules and restrictions would have to be in place?*
- *What kinds of people would be in this world?*
- *How would the people and the world survive?*

Save their reponses. (They'll refer to them in the writing activity.)

▪ Through Ideas

Precision of Language   In the novel, Jonas is chastised for not using precise language; he says "I'm starving" when he really means "I'm hungry." Ask students to think of other phrases in our language that exaggerate and are not precise. Watch as your class really starts to look at language and the power of words.

Community Comparison   Jonas is supposed to live in a perfect community without crime, pain, or unfulfilled needs. How does Jonas's community compare with your community? Challenge students to draw Venn diagrams comparing the two communities. Ask them which community they would rather live in and why.

Chart of the Ceremonies   To keep track of the ceremonies and help students visualize how control is established in the community, we make a chart of the ceremonies on a large piece of butcher paper. We fill in the chart as the ceremonies are revealed in the novel. Then I ask students to make up possible ceremonies and their meanings for the ages that aren't revealed in the book.

Chart of Ceremonies

Ones	– Family Unit/Names given
Twos	
Threes	– Dream telling begins
Fours	
Fives	
Sixes	
Sevens	– Front button jacket/Symbol of Independence
Eights	– No more comfort objects Volunteer hours begin
Nines	– Receive bicycles
Tens	– Haircuts
Elevens	– New undergarments and long pants issued
Twelves	– Assignment

▪ Beyond Ideas

Chapter 24   The ending of *The Giver* tends to leave students a little unsettled. We always have a stimulating discussion about the meaning of the ending. I introduce questions such as the following:

- *What happened to Jonas and*

Gabriel?
- *Is this a historical novel or a futuristic novel?*

My students always have many different opinions, and this leads perfectly to assigning them the task of writing Chapter 24 for the book. Let students tell you how they think the book should have ended. Allow time for everyone to share his or her chapter in class.

■ Writing Idea

After students have read *The Giver*, ask them to read their responses from the Into activity about their visions for a perfect world. After finishing the book, how has that vision changed? What obstacles did they overlook? Is a world without pain a better place to live? Ask them to write what their ideas of a perfect world are now and how such a world could be established.

READING RESPONSE JOURNAL PROMPTS

Chapter 1: Why do you think Jonas is apprehensive about the ceremony of twelve? What do you think the ceremony of twelve is?

Chapter 2: What are your impressions of this community?

Chapter 3: How do the Speakers know when someone breaks a rule? How do you feel about the fact that they announce it to everyone even though they don't mention names?

Chapter 4: How would you feel living in such a structured society? What are the pros and cons?

Chapter 5: Why is it important to stop the stirrings?

Chapter 6: What do you think releasing and Elsewhere mean?

Chapter 7: What can Jonas have done wrong? Why do they skip him?

Chapter 8: Why does Jonas have mixed emotions about his assignment?

Chapter 9: Why is Jonas concerned about some of his new rules?

Chapter 10: Why do you think only one person is allowed to carry the memories of the whole world?

Chapter 11: Why do you think the concept of sameness came about?

Chapter 12: Why would the people relinquish color?

Chapter 13: Is safer better? Tell why or why not.

Chapter 14: Why isn't there pain in Jonas's community? Do you think this is a good idea?

Chapter 15: Why does the Giver ask Jonas to forgive him?

Chapter 16: Why doesn't this society have animals?

Chapter 17: Why doesn't Jonas fit in with his friends anymore?

Chapter 18: Why would the community suffer if Jonas were lost?

Chapter 19: a) Why is Jonas so overwhelmed by finding out what an actual release is? b) Why can Jonas's father release the twin so easily?

Chapter 20: Why does the Giver encourage Jonas to leave?

Chapter 21: Why does Jonas feel the urgency to leave before they had planned?

Chapter 22: How would you feel if you were Jonas right now?

Chapter 23: Why does Jonas feel happy even though he is physically exhausted and hungry? What keeps him going?

Missing May

by Cynthia Rylant

1993 Newbery Medal

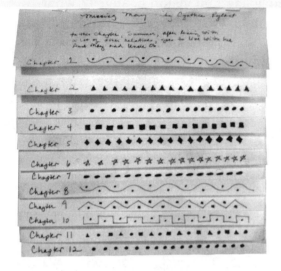

■ Summary

The only real home Summer has ever known is with Aunt May and Uncle Ob. It's a place where she feels loved and comfortable. After her mother died, Summer was passed from relative to relative until Aunt May and Uncle Ob took her in. Six years later, Aunt May dies. Summer and Uncle Ob feel lost and alone. Summer is desperately afraid that she will lose Uncle Ob too. He is so sad, and her presence doesn't seem to be enough to make him want to go on. Then Uncle Ob starts to sense May's spirit and wants to contact her. Oddly enough, it's Cletus, a strange boy from school, who helps Summer and Ob truly grieve for May and gather the strength to go on, even though they are always missing May.

■ Chapter by Chapter

Have your students make a step book for the 12 chapters of *Missing May*. You can follow the instructions given on page 33 of this book. Each student will need six sheets of paper to make the step book.

■ Into Ideas

Interviews   As a class, discuss feelings regarding the death of a loved one. You may want to use some of the following questions:

- *How do people react?*
- *How do they grieve?*
- *What changes in their lives?*
- *What adjustments do they have to make?*

Ask students to think of someone they could interview who has experienced the death of a loved one. Develop interview questions with your class. I always remind my students that this is an extremely sensitive topic. They shouldn't interview someone who is going through the grieving process. They should talk to their parents about the appropriateness of approaching the person they have chosen. Discuss their interviews in class, and have students keep their interviews, as they will need them when you finish reading the book.

Have You Ever . . . ?   Write the following "Have you ever . . . ?" questions on the board.

> Have you ever . . .
>   felt all alone?
>   experienced the death of a loved one?
>   felt responsible for an older person?
>   been optimistic?
>   been pessimistic?
>   not told your parents the whole truth?
>   experienced mood swings?
>   kept your feelings to yourself?
>   had a major change in your family?
>   believed in something you could not see, hear, or touch?

Go over the questions with your students. Then form small groups, and ask them to respond to two of the questions. One response can be private, but they should share the other response with the group. Students will do a five-minute quick-write on each of their two questions. I find it helpful to call time after the first five minutes and start the class together on the second question. The group then discusses the respons-

es. At the end of the exercise, tell your students that they all have something in common with Summer since she experiences all these things in *Missing May*.

■ Through Ideas

Character Webs   As the students are reading *Missing May*, have them make character webs. They start with the title of the book in the center of the web and then branch out with the characters as they encounter them in the book. Each character should have distinguishing characteristics around his or her name. This assignment continues to grow throughout the book.

Character Collages   Ask your students to create collages for the main characters in the book (May, Ob, Summer, and Cletus). They should create symbols to form the base for their collages. For example, May's symbol could be an angel. A student would then cut out a tagboard angel for the base of the collage. He or she would cut out from magazines words and images that reflect May's life, and paste them onto a piece of tagboard. The student would follow these directions for the remaining three characters. This is an assignment that will continue throughout the novel.

Letters to May   Require each student to write five letters to May. Two letters will be from Summer, two from Ob, and one from Cletus. Students should select the points in the novel where they want to write these letters. Remind students to take on the persona of the character in the letters.

■ Beyond Activities

Interpretive Posters *Missing May* is written in two parts, "Still as the Night" and "Set Free." Ask students to divide a large piece of poster or construction paper in half by drawing a line down the middle. One half should be titled "Still as the Night" and the other half should be titled "Set Free." Under each title, students should draw pictures or symbols from the book that reflect each title and then explain why the author gave the title to each section.

■ Writing Idea

Students will use the information they gathered in their interviews of people who have experienced the death of a loved one, and what they have learned from the characters in *Missing May,* to write essays about the effects of the death of a loved one on the survivors. Students should include the stages of grief and adjustment and explore coping mechanisms. Encourage them to do research on the Internet or in the library. Guide students in their writing so they can bring a full picture of loss as Cynthia Rylant did. Emphasize that they should try to end on a positive note by recounting the influence that the person had on the lives of the survivors.

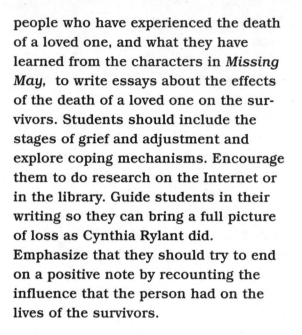

READING RESPONSE JOURNAL PROMPTS

Chapter 1: "Whirligigs of Fire and Dreams, glistening Coke bottles and chocolate milk cartons to greet me. I was six years old and I had come home." Explain what Summer means by this statement.

Chapter 2: Why is May so important to Summer and Ob? Why is Summer upset that Ob says that May felt like she did when "we was packing up to go to Ohio"?

Chapter 3: Summer, Ob, and Cletus depend on each other in different ways. Explain each character's needs and how they fill those needs for each other. How does May fit into the picture?

Chapter 4: How does Cletus give Ob hope?

Chapter 5: Why is Summer so worried about Ob? How are her own fears connected with Ob's?

Chapter 6: Why does Summer still have hope for Ob?

Chapter 7: Compare and contrast Summer's and Cletus's outlooks on life, and more specifically their outlooks on Ob's situation. Do you think one person's outlook is better than the other's? Explain.

Chapter 8: a) Why does Ob feel it necessary to avoid telling the Underwoods "the real truth" about why they are going to Putnam County? b) What is the "something else" that Summer and Ob feel when they leave the Underwoods' home?

Chapter 9: How are Summer, Ob, and Cletus like three visitors heading for Oz?

Chapter 10: Make a graph of the characters' moods from the beginning of Chapter 10 to the end. Describe the mood changes and their causes.

Chapter 11: a) Why does the owl flying over the trailer finally release Summer's tears for May? b) Why were May, Ob, and Summer such a good family?

Chapter 12: Why does Ob decide to put his Whirligigs in May's garden?

Shiloh

by Phyllis Reynolds Naylor

1992 Newbery Medal

Shiloh
by Phyllis Reynolds Naylor

Chapter 1

While walking in the hills near his home, Marty Preston sees a sad beagle near the old Shiloh schoolhouse. The dog follows Marty home. Marty names the dog Shiloh and hopes his father will let him keep him.

VOCABULARY

belches	commences
decency	envy
jowls	moody
nourish	omission
pneumonia	quavery
suspicious	

■ Summary

This story takes place in the hills of West Virginia. Eleven-year-old Marty Preston finds a young beagle that he feels sure has been abused. The beagle follows Marty home, and he names it Shiloh. Marty's parents make him return Shiloh to Judd, the abusive owner, but Marty thinks of a plan to keep Shiloh away from his cruel owner. This is a heartwarming story that encourages readers to think about right and wrong and the overwhelming power of love and kindness.

■ Chapter by Chapter

I pair students, and have each pair take one chapter of the book. After we have read a chapter, the assigned partners create a shoe box diorama depicting a scene from that chapter. The diorama is accompanied by a 3 by 5 card summarizing the chapter. I display these dioramas in order around the classroom as a reminder of how the story unfolds.

■ Into Ideas

"Rex" by James Thurber   The short story "Rex" by James Thurber is a great dog story that students really enjoy reading. We discuss pets and

people's love for pets and how the animals should be cared for. I always enjoy reading a short story with my students as a jumping off point for a new novel. It is also the perfect time to talk to students about different genres of literature and encourage them to read in areas that really interest them.

Pet Reports   Most students have pets of their own or have had pets at one time. They are really excited when I ask them to do a short oral report on their pets. I tell students to show us pictures of their pets (I haven't been brave enough to let them bring their pets to class yet!), tell us how they got their pets, how they care for the animals, and what their pets mean to them. I limit the oral reports to 3–5 minutes. It lets everyone feel excited about sharing something so close to them and reminds students how special their pets are to them. This is especially important for them to keep prominently in mind as we read *Shiloh* so that they can really understand how Marty feels. Occasionally I will have a student who doesn't have a pet and has never had one; I have always found that their grandparents or neighbors have pets that they have had special times with, and I encourage them to report on those pets.

■ Through Ideas

Marty's Journal   Marty is unable to tell anyone about his secret, yet he is dying to tell someone. He also has mixed emotions about what he is doing, especially about keeping things

from his parents. Encourage students to pretend that they are Marty and keep personal journals throughout this book. They can write how Marty might feel, the questions and fears he might have, his dreams, and so on. Tell students to write in their journals after each chapter.

Tableaux   Tableau is a dramatic technique used to encourage students to put themselves in a character's place. I have groups of students act out specific scenes in *Shiloh* and then infer what the character is thinking. Begin by writing several poignant scenes on 3 by 5 cards, such as the following:

- Shiloh follows Marty home for the first time.
- Marty's parents tell him he must give Shiloh back to Judd.
- Marty gives Shiloh back to Judd.
- Shiloh returns to Marty.
- Marty hides Shiloh.
- Marty plays with Shiloh in the hideout.
- Ma finds out about Shiloh.
- What happens after the German Shepherd attacks Shiloh.
- Judd comes back for his dog.
- Marty sees Judd kill a doe out of season.

Distribute one index card to each group of students (group size will depend on the number of actors required for each scene). Ask students to act out their scenes and then freeze at the climax. Tap one student at a time to "unfreeze" him or her. The student then talks and acts like the character and relates how he or she feels at this particular moment. If you tap the student again, he or she must freeze again. Continue this until all the characters have had a chance to speak.

■ Beyond Ideas

Continue the Story Ask students to write additional chapters of the novel, paying particular attention to what will happen to the relationship between Marty and Judd.

■ Writing Idea

Ask students to write about memorable experiences they have had with animals. This should not be a report on a favorite animal but a memoir of a time with an animal. The animal could be someone's pet; it could be a bird that flew out of the sky and stole a baseball cap off someone's head; or a happening at the zoo. Remind students that they want their readers to feel like they were there at the time, too. Encourage them to focus on setting and emotions, and to fully describe the characters involved.

READING RESPONSE JOURNAL PROMPTS

Chapter 1: Why does Marty think Shiloh hasn't been treated well?

Chapter 2: How would you feel if you had to take Shiloh to Judd and leave him there?

Chapter 3: Why doesn't Judd name his dogs?

Chapter 4: Why does Marty get a full night's sleep for the first time in a long time?

Chapter 5: Should Marty give Shiloh back to Judd? Explain your thinking.

Chapter 6: a) How does Marty feel about lying? b) Why do you think Judd is so mean?

Chapter 7: How would you feel if you were Marty?

Chapter 8: What do you think will happen next?

Chapter 9: Describe how Marty is feeling right now.

Chapter 10: What's right in this situation?

Chapter 11: Create a plan to help Marty keep Shiloh.

Chapter 12: What would you do now if you were Marty?

Chapter 13: Predict what will happen next.

Chapter 14: a) Why does Marty feel taller than he really is next to Judd? b) What do you think of Marty's bargain with Judd? Will it work?

Chapter 15: What makes Judd change?

Maniac Magee
by Jerry Spinelli

1991 Newbery Winner

■ Summary

Maniac Magee is the story of Jeffrey, a young boy orphaned at the age of three. He is sent to live with his aunt and uncle who hate each other. Jeffrey, dubbed Maniac, puts up with his relatives' separate lives for eight years and then runs away. The story follows Jeffrey as he survives on the run. Along the way, he meets good and bad people and influences both. Jeffrey gains a reputation as he dares to cross over to the East End. He tries to make others understand that people are the same, no matter what color their skin is.

■ Chapter by Chapter

I ask my students to do pictorial timelines of Maniac Magee's life. I present them with several examples of timelines and discuss each one. I then have students brainstorm the important events

VOCABULARY

abruptly	accurate
befuddled	blemished
contortions	finicky
grungy	hallucination
hoisted	incubating
instincts	lambasting
languished	meandering
mirage	nonchalantly
ornery	pandemonium
paralyzed	perilous
preposterous	repertoire
replicas	reprisals
robust	stoic
suffice	vanished

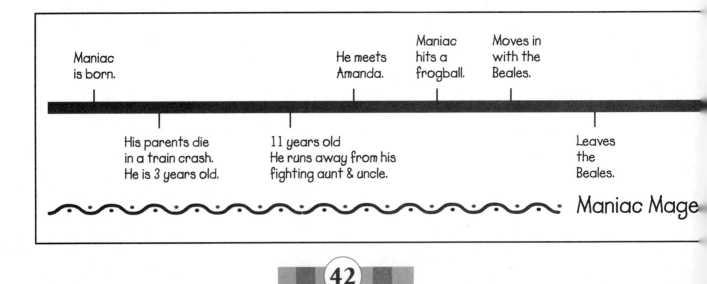

Maniac is born.

His parents die in a train crash. He is 3 years old.

He meets Amanda.

11 years old
He runs away from his fighting aunt & uncle.

Maniac hits a frogball.

Moves in with the Beales.

Leaves the Beales.

Maniac Mage

in Maniac's life and write them in chronological order. Then they fold $8\frac{1}{2}$ by 11–inch paper in half lengthwise like a hot dog, cut it in half, and then tape the two pieces together, end to end, to form one long timeline. Students draw a thick, solid line lengthwise along the center of the timeline. The events shoot off from this center line; positive events go above the line and negative events go below the line. Each event should have a caption and a picture.

Into Ideas

Introducing the Character   Read the "Before the Story" section of *Maniac Magee* with your students. Discuss the section, and ask students to list what they think they know about Maniac from this section. Make sure they touch upon the following areas:

- personality
- talents
- neighborhood
- family life
- legend
- questions this passage creates

Write students' responses on a large chart. Keep the chart up and confirm or refute students' conjectures as you read the story.

Through Ideas

Chapter Titles   Since this story has no chapter titles, you can ask your students to create titles for each chapter. This is a fun and challenging activity for them to do. I always ask everyone to share their chapter titles at the beginning of the next class. This takes a very short amount of time, but as students hear others' chapter titles, it helps to improve the creativity and quality of the next day's chapter titles.

Cross-Age Tutoring   Maniac uses several picture books to help Grayson learn to read. I bring in these books which include *Lyle, Lyle Crocodile*; *The Story of Babar*; *Mike Mulligan's Steam Shovel*; and *The Little Engine That Could*. I then arrange to take my class to a primary classroom to have my students

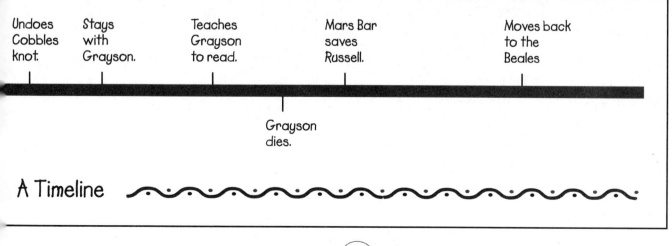

Undoes Cobbles knot.   Stays with Grayson.   Teaches Grayson to read.   Mars Bar saves Russell.   Moves back to the Beales

Grayson dies.

A Timeline

read to and read with the younger students who are just learning to read. Each of my students brings two picture books to read to their cross-age buddies. It is great to see my students sprawled out on the floor of the children's section of our public library and reading to find just the right books to share with their younger buddies. This experience gives my students a lot of self confidence and an appreciation of what is involved in teaching someone to read.

Four Homes   Maniac stays in four different homes in the book—the Beales', the Pickwells', the McNabs', and Earl Grayson's. I ask my students to draw pictures and descriptions of each home. I then ask them to write about which home they would have chosen to live in and why.

■ Beyond Ideas

Plan to End Prejudice   Prejudice is a theme that runs throughout this novel. I ask my students to share times when they experienced prejudice and how they felt about it. I also ask them to interview someone who has been a victim of prejudice. Students report orally on these incidents to give the class a broader view of how prejudice affects our society. I then challenge them to come up with a plan to end prejudice.

■ Writing Idea

Encourage students to research organizations that reach out to homeless people and then write about them.

READING RESPONSE JOURNAL PROMPTS

Chapter 1: How does the legend of Maniac begin?

Chapter 2: What is the lost year?

Chapter 3: Why does Jeffrey Magee pick Amanda to talk to?

Chapter 4: What new talents of Jeffrey's do you find out about in this chapter?

Chapter 5: How does Jeffrey show compassion and bravery in this chapter?

Chapter 6: How does Jeffrey get food?

Chapter 7: Why is McNab so angry with Jeffrey?

Chapter 8: Why does everyone call Jeffrey "Maniac"?

Chapter 9: Predict what will happen to Jeffrey in the East End.

Chapter 10: What does Maniac feel like doing at the end of the chapter?

Chapter 11: Why does Amanda trust Jeffrey and not Mars Bar?

Chapter 12: Why does Jeffrey smile?

Chapter 13: How do things change at the Beale house?

Chapter 14: Why does Jeffrey love his new life?

Chapter 15: Why does Jeffrey hug Mrs. Beale when she slaps his trash-talking mouth?

Chapter 16: How does Jeffrey figure out he isn't really white?

Chapter 17: Why can't Maniac sleep?

Chapter 18: What do you think Cobble's Knot is?

Chapter 19: Will the knot be the answer to Maniac's problems?

Chapter 20: Why is Maniac able to undo the knot when no one else can?

Chapter 21: Why does Maniac leave the Beales?

Chapter 22: Why doesn't Grayson take Jeffrey to some official place?

Chapter 23: What notion do you think Grayson has?

Chapter 24: What does Jeffrey teach Grayson?

Chapter 25: Why does Grayson think he has no stories to tell?

Chapter 26: How do Maniac and Grayson learn from each other?

Chapter 27: Why is Maniac able to teach Grayson to read?

Chapter 28: Why does Grayson finally feel unburdened?

Chapter 29: Why does Maniac paint the number 101 outside the bandshell?

Chapter 30: Why are Maniac and Grayson so ambitious with their Christmas decorations?

Chapter 31: Why is this Christmas special for Grayson and Jeffrey?

Chapter 32: Why is Maniac running again?

Chapter 33: Why is Maniac waiting for death?

Chapter 34: Why does Maniac decide to get up and do something? What does this say about him as a person?

Chapter 35: What does Maniac mean when he thinks "Who's the orphan here, anyway?"

Chapter 36: What truly makes Russell and Piper go to school?

Chapter 37: Will Maniac go back into the East End? Explain why or why not.

Chapter 38: Why is Jeffrey embarrassed?

Chapter 39: What is the new smell in the McNab house?

Chapter 40: Why does Maniac continue to stay involved with the NcNabs?

Chapter 41: How does Maniac try to bring the west and east sides together?

Chapter 42: Why does Maniac bring Mars Bar to the west side?

Chapter 43: Why doesn't Maniac go live with the Beales or Pickwells?

Chapter 44: What's wrong with Maniac?

Chapter 45: What's happening to Mars Bar?

Chapter 46: Why do Amanda and Mars Bars go get Maniac?

The True Confessions of Charlotte Doyle
by Avi

1991 Newbery Honor Book

■ Summary

Miss Charlotte Doyle boards the ship the *Seahawk* for her journey to America. She is sailing alone to meet her family after completing studies at the Barrington School for Better Girls in England. Two families are to accompany Charlotte on the trip, but both families are scared off by tales of a cruel captain and a mutinous crew. Charlotte begins an incredible voyage where she goes from passenger to crew. She endures many hardships—including being accused of murder!

■ Chapter by Chapter

I ask my students to do their chapter by chapter project in the form of a ship's log. We talk about the fact that the captain of a ship keeps a daily log of everything that happens on the ship during the day. Ships' logs always contain dates and times and are an accurate account of everything that happens on the voyage. I have my students pretend that they are either Charlotte or Captain Jaggery and keep a ship's log from that perspective. Depending of their choice of character, the tone of the logs will be very different. Students make at least one entry into their logs for each chapter.

VOCABULARY

agitated	agog
amputated	apparition
audacity	beguile
blatant	censure
chaos	complicity
decrepit	dirk
doldrums	impertinence
malicious	naive
punctilious	quell
restitution	reticule
sallow	sardonic
stiletto	trepidation
vexation	

■ Into Ideas

An Important Warning   I read to my class Charlotte's important warning that appears at the beginning of this book. We discuss and react to the warning, thereby setting the stage for what's to come.

Appendix   I also have my students look at the appendix of the book prior to reading it. The appendix has a lot of technical information about ships and things that Charlotte will refer to in the

book. I do not know a lot about ships and many times found myself flipping to the appendix to clarify something. Students may not be as willing to flip back when they need to, so I have the class create large posters of the two diagrams in the appendix to display in front of the room. This way all they have to do is look at the posters if they are unsure where the mainmast is, for example. Students also become familiar with the terms as they draw the posters. Maybe you know the theory of how you can forget your grocery list but still remember what you need when you go to the store because you made a list in the first place. The same general idea applies here.

I also have students practice ship's time. We copy the chart to put up in front of the room. Then I let them take turns ringing a bell to see if everyone can figure out what time it is.

■ Through Ideas

Quick Write   I ask students to react to this quote from page 37: "Justice is poorly served when you speak ill of your betters." This reaction takes the form of a quick write, which means students have approximately five minutes to write what they are thinking. The students' pens or pencils must move the entire five minutes even if they are writing "I don't know what to write." I find that they would rather write something on the topic than "I don't know what to write." This takes care of any problems with students writing one sentence and saying "I'm

done." After the five minutes, I ask for volunteers to share their responses, and a discussion ensues.

Venn Diagrams   The book is spilt into two parts. Charlotte changes a great deal from Part I to Part II. I ask students to make Venn diagrams showing those differences as well as how she remains the same.

■ Beyond Ideas

Interior Monologues   I ask students to deliver interior monologues as if they are characters in the book and talk about their lives, feelings, and/or experiences. A perfect place for an interior monologue in this novel is at the end. Ask students to write interior monologues from the viewpoint of Charlotte's father as he reads her diary. How does he feel about, react to, and deal with his daughter's diary? Remind students that these are his thoughts, not what he finally decides to share with Charlotte.

Quick Write   As another five-minute quick write, have students put themselves in Charlotte's place. Could they have done what she did? After all they had been through, would they have gone back? Ask them to explain why or why not.

■ Writing Idea

Challenge students to support or deny the following statement: Charlotte's father really loves her. Tell them to be sure to use facts from the novel to support their theses.

READING RESPONSE JOURNAL PROMPTS

Chapter 1: What would you do if you were Charlotte? How would you feel?

Chapter 2: Why does everyone dislike Captain Jaggery? What is his plan and how does it involve Charlotte?

Chapter 3: How does meeting Captain Jaggery change Charlotte?

Chapter 4: Why does Charlotte need the dirk?

Chapter 5: Why does Captain Jaggery warn Charlotte of the round robin?

Chapter 6: What do you think will happen next?

Chapter 7: Why are both Captain Jaggery and Mr. Zachariah courting Charlotte's friendship?

Chapter 8: Do you think Captain Jaggery is a good leader? Back up your decision.

Chapter 9: What would you have done if you were Charlotte?

Chapter 10: Do you think Charlotte's opinion of the Captain has changed? Tell why or why not.

Chapter 11: Describe Charlotte's feelings.

Chapter 12: Why does Charlotte want to become one of the crew?

Chapter 13: How do you think the Captain will handle Charlotte's decision?

Chapter 14: How does Charlotte gain the respect of her crew mates?

Chapter 15: Why doesn't the Captain want to avoid the hurricane?

Chapter 16: How can Zachariah still be alive?

Chapter 17: Who do you think killed Mr. Hollybrass and why?

Chapter 18: What is the difference between unnatural and unusual as Charlotte sees it?

Chapter 19: How will Charlotte and Zachariah get out of their predicament?

Chapter 20: Why is Captain Jaggery waiting for Charlotte?

Chapter 21: Why doesn't the crew help Charlotte?

Chapter 22: Why does Charlotte choose to go back to the *Seahawk*?

Number the Stars
by Lois Lowry

1990 Newbery Medal

■ Summary

Ten-year-old Annemarie Johansen lives in Copenhagen in 1943. For the past three years, the Nazis have occupied Denmark. Like other Danes, Annemarie is having a hard time getting used to the changes; there are curfews and soldiers on the streets and supplies are low. But nothing prepares her for what comes next—Denmark's Jews are to be "relocated." Annemarie's best friend, Ellen, is Jewish. The Johansens hide Ellen at Uncle Henrik's coastal farm. Annemarie learns that her uncle, her sister's fiancee—and now she and her family—are part of the Danish Resistance, a group that smuggles Danish Jews safely to neutral Sweden. *Number the Stars* is a story of bravery and true love for what is right.

■ Chapter by Chapter

Symbolism is used throughout this novel and is an important concept to teach students. I ask students to do symbolic posters for their chapter by chapter. After reading each chapter, they choose symbols to represent the chapter and then write why they chose it. For example, after reading Chapter 1, a student might choose a cupcake as a symbol. The students would draw the cupcake and explain that he or she chose this symbol because it repre-sents all the changes that have taken place in Copenhagen during the Nazi occupation. For instance, the girls dream of cupcakes, and their parents dream of even greater changes.

VOCABULARY

belligerently	civilized
dawdled	defiantly
disdainfully	imperious
intricate	obstinate
permeated	protruding
quavering	residential
sabotage	sarcastically
sulking	swastika
tension	torment
trousseau	

■ Into Ideas

Background Knowledge Students are going to need some background knowledge of World War II, the Nazis, and the plight of the Jewish people at that time. You can give them the information they need, but I have always found it more effective to bring in a guest speaker who experienced World War II. Ask them to explain to the students what was happening to Jewish people at that time; it carries more weight than a teacher's lecture.

Map of Europe I hand out an outline map of Europe, and ask students to fill in the countries, focusing special attention on the countries mentioned in the novel. They keep their maps in their Reading Response Journals for handy reference throughout the novel.

Denmark I ask students to do some quick research on Denmark and bring it in to share informally with the rest of the class. I have them look particularly for information on King Christian, Denmark during World War II, a detailed map of Denmark, and the Danish Resistance movement. We share this information in class so that students have a little background knowledge as they read the novel.

■ Through Ideas

Star of David I contact a Jewish organization or a synagogue to invite a speaker to come to the classroom and share the importance of the Star of David. I then have a discussion with students about symbols and their importance. They are asked to draw symbols that have special importance to them. Students display their symbols and do short essays about what the symbols mean to them.

Filmstrips I divide the 17 chapters among pairs of students and have each pair create a filmstrip for one chapter. Students are asked to break down their chapter into its eight most significant details or events. Have pairs make their filmstrips by taping together eight sheets of black construction paper to form a flimstrip. In the middle of each sheet of construction paper, they glue a sheet of plain white paper to make a filmstrip box. In each flimstrip box, they illustrate and write a small caption for each detail. The events must be in chronological order so that the filmstrip could run just as a film would. It must depict the chapter from start to finish. Display the filmstrips in chapter order for a great "film" review of the book.

■ Beyond Ideas

A Wartime Newspaper Have students create a newspaper for the time period in the book. They can choose to do an underground newspaper or a conventional newspaper. I usually place my students in groups of four to six for this activity. Everything about their newspapers must revolve around the time period, characters, and events of the novel. Each group must include as many actual parts of a newspaper as possible. Review the parts of a newspaper with students: advertisements, arts and entertainment, business, classified ads, comics, daily living (advice, fashion, education), editorials, letters to the editor, features, front page, lead story, movie guide, obituaries, sports, stock market, and weather.

I require my students to have at least one hard news story per person in the group. Hard news stories are defined as lead stories, feature stories, and editorials. Each student must also contribute at least one other type of story. I bring in several newspapers so that they can see the layout and content. I also remind my students of the 5 W's of newspaper writing: who, what, where, when, and why. I encourage them to search the Internet for information regarding the time period and costs of products.

■ Writing Idea

Read the Afterword with your students, and then ask them how the letter excerpt from Kim Malthe-Bruun makes them feel. Have them write essays that show how they would apply his words to our society and our world.

READING RESPONSE JOURNAL PROMPTS

Chapter 1: Why is it important to be one of the crowd in Copenhagen?

Chapter 2: Why has the whole world changed?

Chapter 3: Why is Annemarie frightened?

Chapter 4: a) Why do the Danes blow up their own naval fleet?
b) Why does Ellen have to pretend to be Annemarie's sister?

Chapter 5: How would you feel if you were Ellen?

Chapter 6: Why is Papa speaking in code to Henrik? What is it all about?

Chapter 7: Why is there no laughter between Mama and her brother?

Chapter 8: Why are they making up the story of Aunt Birte?

Chapter 9: a) How brave are you? Put yourself in Annemarie's or Ellen's place.
b) Why do they stage Great-Aunt Birte's death?

Chapter 10: Predict what it is time for.

Chapter 11: What part of the Rosens' pride are the German soldiers unable to take away?

Chapter 12: What happens to Mama?

Chapter 13: Why is it better if Annemarie doesn't know what is in the package? What can be so important that Mama would put Annemarie in danger?

Chapter 14: Why does Annemarie think of stories on her trip to the boat?

Chapter 15: Why do the soldiers let Annemarie go?

Chapter 16: a) How do all of Annemarie's "ifs" save the Rosens' lives?
b) Why are Lise and Peter willing to risk their lives for the Resistance movement?

Chapter 17: What really happened to Lise?

Hatchet
by Gary Paulsen

1988 Newbery Honor Book

■ Summary

Thirteen-year-old Brian Robeson is flying in a single-engine plane to visit his father. Suddenly the pilot has a heart attack, and the plane crashes in the Canadian Wilderness. Brian is left alone with few materials to help him survive and the terrible thoughts of The Secret and his parents' divorce. Realizing that he must rely on himself to survive, Brian pushes self-pity aside. His story is a remarkable tale of survival spanning 54 days.

■ Chapter by Chapter

Students enjoy making little books to keep track of the action in *Hatchet*. A detailed description of how to make little books is given on page 25 of this book (the **Chapter by Chapter** project for *The Midwife's Apprentice*) .

■ Into Ideas

Jigsawing Information and the Internet   There are five topics in *Hatchet* that I want my students to have some knowledge of—1) heart attacks, 2) small airplanes, 3) amphibious planes, 4) the north woods of Canada, and 5) Gary Paulsen. I divide my class into five groups of five. Each student receives a construction-paper card with a number from 1 to 5 written on it. These numbers correspond to the top-

VOCABULARY

altimeter	amphibious
corrosive	dormant
exasperation	furor
haunches	incessant
infuriating	oblivious
persistent	pitiful
pulverized	regulate
sarcasm	stymied
tendrils	viciously

ics listed above. For five groups I use five different colors of construction paper; for example, five orange squares will be numbered 1, 2, 3, 4, 5, five green squares will be numbered 1, 2, 3, 4, 5, and so on. The color groups are called Home groups, and the number groups are called Expert groups.

Before class begins, I make five tents out of the different colors of construction paper. Underneath each tent, I write a different number from 1 to 5. As students walk into class, I hand out the construction-paper cards and ask them to sit at the table that has the same color tent as their card. Each group should have the numbers 1, 2, 3, 4, and 5 at its table. I tell students that this is their Home group. At this point,

I ask students to look at the numbers underneath their construction-paper tents. Then I instruct them to look at their cards and move to the table that has that number tent. I tell students that this is their Expert group. I give each group its topic. They will work in these groups today to find out information about their topics. Tomorrow they will be responsible for reporting on this topic to their Home groups. I take my students to the school's computer lab, and direct them to research their topics on the Internet. Although they are working as groups to find information about their topics, each individual can search different places on the Internet. The groups then compile the information to share with their Home groups the next day.

Students return to their Home groups the following day. Each member reports what they learned about the topic. Remember that you will have five different groups doing the same thing. Remind students to take notes for future reference. In this way, your class has learned about topics important to the novel, yet everyone has done research on only one topic. And it has only taken two class periods! Your students have been responsible for their own learning, too.

■ Through Ideas

Mini-Reports Brian refers to many different plants and animals that students may not be familiar with, so I assign mini-reports to help them gain a better understanding of these things. A mini-report consists of a picture of the plant or animal and a short written description. Students present their mini-reports to the class. Then I post the mini-reports for students to refer to when something comes up in the story that they may have forgotten. Topics for these mini-reports include chokecherries and hazelnut bushes, snowshoe and cottontail rabbits, ruffed grouse, bluegills, sunfish, perch, snapping turtles, timber wolves, and moose.

A Letter from Mom or Dad For this activity, I ask students to pretend that they are either Brian's mom or his dad. They write letters to Brian when the search for him has finally been officially terminated—one month after he was reported missing. Remind students that Brian's parents think they will never see their son again so their letters are a way for them to reach out to him.

■ Beyond Ideas

Paper Bag Reports I have students take ordinary lunch bags and draw scenes from the novel on the front of the bags. The front of the bag should have the title and author as well as the student's name. On the back of the paper bag, they write the name(s) of the main characters, supporting characters,

the setting(s), conflict(s), and resolution(s). Inside the bag, students should place at least eight objects that represent significant events in the novel or aspects of the characters' personalities. At least four of the objects must be handmade by the students. When they bring their bags to class, I have students share their bags in small groups. This is a fun and helpful way for students to review the important aspects of the novel. Because they have put a lot of time and energy into this assignment, I have them take a "museum" walk to view all the other bags in the classroom. We don't have time for all the students to share their bags, but I use this "museum" walk idea often to validate everyone's work and to allow the students to show their talents to the whole class.

■ Writing Idea

I tell my students to imagine that they are Brian. He's just been asked to write a short article for *People* magazine about his ordeal. I remind them that *People* magazine articles must be interesting immediately or readers will just skip to the next story about their favorite celebrity. As Brian, they can give details about what happened. The editors pose these questions to Brian:

- *What kind of person survives a plane crash and then manages to survive alone in the wilderness for 54 days?*
- *Where did you get your strength and resolve?*

READING RESPONSE JOURNAL PROMPTS

Chapter 1: What would you do if you were Brian? How would you feel?

Chapter 2: Describe what Brian is feeling as he tries to get in touch with someone by radio.

Chapter 3: a) What is the color that came?
b) Explain what the last word in the chapter means.

Chapter 4: Why does Brian think he is unlucky?

Chapter 5: Why is Brian fighting panic?

Chapter 6: How would you have found food and shelter if you were Brian?

Chapter 7: Why is Brian overcome with self-pity?

Chapter 8: Why does Brian have the dream?

Chapter 9: Why does Brian call fire his friend?

Chapter 10: Why is hope important to Brian?

Chapter 11: Why does Brian keep saying "There were these things to do"?

Chapter 12: Explain Brian's feelings right now.

Chapter 13: How is the new Brian different from the old Brian?

Chapter 14: How does Brian learn from his mistakes?

Chapter 15: Why does first meat taste so good?

Chapter 16: Why is it important for Brian to be tough in the head?

Chapter 17: Why is Brian trying so hard to get into the plane?

Chapter 18: Why is the hatchet so important?

Chapter 19: Why does Brian react to the bush pilot the way he does?

Epilogue: How does Brian's experience change his life even after he is rescued?

The Whipping Boy
by Sid Fleischman

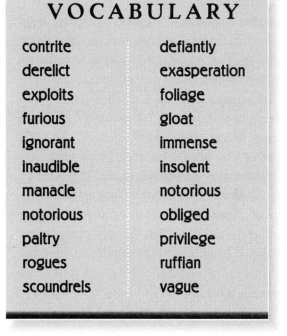

■ Summary

Prince Horace, better known as Prince Brat, is notorious for his awful behavior. This is a particular problem for Jemmy, who is literally the prince's whipping boy. Jemmy receives all of Prince Brat's whippings because no one is allowed to whip a prince. When the Prince decides to run away, he takes Jemmy with him. Neither boy likes the other, but through run-ins with ruffians, they learn to appreciate each other and become friends.

■ Chapter by Chapter

Because this book is so short, instead of doing a chapter by chapter assign-ment, I have students do an overall pro-ject. I ask them to cover cereal boxes with plain paper. They can wrap the boxes just like presents. On the front of the box goes the title, the author's name, a drawing of a scene, and a short summary of the book. On a side panel goes a list of the characters and a description of each one. A review of the book appears on the other side panel. On the back of the box, a game based on the book appears. The game can have any format that students choose, but it should contain details relevant to the book. Students write their names on the top of the boxes.

■ Into Ideas

Story Impression   You can do this activity in one of three ways. The first choice is to write the title of the book on the board and then ask students to write stories using this title. After students share their stories, keep them on hand. When students finish reading *The Whipping Boy*, they can see if anyone was on the right track. The second method is to write all the chapter titles of the book on the board and then have students write stories based on that information. The final way is to write the first line of *The Whipping Boy* on the board: "The young Prince was known here and there (and just about everywhere else) as Prince Brat." Ask students to write stories using that as the first line. They always come up with some really fun stories, and the stories help them to keep a running dialogue with the text as they read and then check their stories with Sid Fleischman's.

■ Through Ideas

Comic Strips   There are many comical, fun scenes in *The Whipping Boy*. I ask my students to choose a scene from the first half of the book to make into a comic strip. The comic strips must be at least five frames long. I bring in several samples of comic strips so that students can get the idea of the flow of the strips and the way thoughts and dialogue are presented. I also ask students to choose a scene from the second half of the book to portray in comic-strip style.

Readers Theaters   Chapter 11 is the perfect place to have students create a readers theater. Students script the chapter by designating one speaker for each character and one narrator for each character. Give them examples of how to format the script so that it is clear when each character and narrator speaks. Show students that characters only say what is contained within quotation marks and their narrators say everything else. Remind them that the best readers theater scripts are those that have a balance of dialogue and narration. You can take this a step further by asking students to find other places where a readers theater might be successful.

■ Beyond Ideas

New Verses to the Ballad   Throughout the novel, we hear several verses of the "Ballad of Hold-Your-Nose Billy and Cutwater." Ask your students to write the final verses for this ballad now that the story is done. If any of your students are really into music, it is fun to ask them to set the ballad to music and sing their final verses.

Video Comparisons   Show a video that features switching roles, such as "Freaky Friday" or "Like Father, Like Son," and ask students to compare how *The Whipping Boy* handled switching roles to how the video handles the situation.

■ Writing Idea

Ask your students to pretend that they are Prince Horace at the end of the novel and have them write letters of recommendation to the King about Jemmy.

READING RESPONSE JOURNAL PROMPTS

Chapter 1: Why doesn't Jemmy bawl when he is whipped?

Chapter 2: What do you think of the practice of keeping whipping boys?

Chapter 3: Why doesn't Prince Brat have any friends?

Chapter 4: What do you think the cutthroats will do with them?

Chapter 5: How does Prince Brat make the situation worse?

Chapter 6: Why do Hold-Your-Nose-Billy and Cutwater think they're rich?

Chapter 7: Why do the ruffians decide that Jemmy is the Prince?

Chapter 8: What is Jemmy up to?

Chapter 9: Why might the ruffians fall for Jemmy's plan?

Chapter 10: Why won't Jemmy's plan work?

Chapter 11: How does Jemmy get around the Prince's refusal to cooperate with the plan?

Chapter 12: Why can't Jemmy trust the Prince for protection?

Chapter 13: Why is Jemmy speechless?

Chapter 14: Why doesn't the Prince want to go back home?

Chapter 15: Why doesn't Jemmy leave the Prince behind?

Chapter 16: Why can't Jemmy feel satisfaction when the Prince gets whipped?

Chapter 17: Why do the Prince and Jemmy feel safe now?

Chapter 18: Why is Jemmy confused about his feelings for Prince Brat?

Chapter 19: How has the Prince changed?

Chapter 20: Why does Jemmy trust the Prince?

Sarah, Plain and Tall
by Patricia MacLachlan

1986 Newbery Medal

■ Summary

Mr. Witting needs a wife for himself and a mother for his children. The trouble is that he and his children live and farm in a very remote area, and it's a hard and lonely life. When Mr. Witting decides to advertise for a wife, Sarah answers his ad. Through a series of letters, Sarah and the Wittings come to know each other. Sarah comes and visits for a trial period, and the desire for her to be part of the family grows even stronger.

■ Chapter by Chapter

I have students do a wheel book for this novel. You will need two pieces of manila tagboard cut in nine-inch-diameter circles. Place the two circles on top of each other and poke a hole through the centers of both circles. Insert a brad through the holes to secure the circles together. The brad also allows the circles to turn independently of each other. Students divide the bottom circle into eight equal pieces like a pie. (I have my students take their wheels apart to do all their work and then reassemble them.) In each slice of the pie, they draw a picture and write a short summary of each chapter. This will be done for Chapters 1–8. The top piece of the wheel then

VOCABULARY

collapsed	dusk
feisty	fetch
hollow	paddock
pesky	primly
pungent	sly
stubbornly	whickering
wretched	

has one 1/8 slice of pie cut out of it. This enables students to turn the outer wheel and see one section of the bottom wheel at a time. The outer wheel contains the title, the author's name, the student's name, and a picture of the last chapter of the book—Chapter 9.

■ Into Ideas

Poetry   Ask students to write cinquains—five line stanzas—about a favorite relative or a family friend using the following pattern:

Noun
Adjective, Adjective
–ing verb, –ing verb, –ing verb
Four-word free statement
Synonym for the noun.

■ Through Ideas

Write an Advertisement   Mr. Witting advertises for a wife in *Sarah, Plain and Tall*. Have students pretend that they are Mr. Witting and write advertisements for a wife. Urge them to consider how to word the ads to attract the kind of person the Wittings want.

Seashells and Flowers   Sarah talks about all kinds of seashells with the children. I ask students to bring in any shells they have (we live very near the coast) to share, and we look up the different kinds in a reference book. We try to find all the shells mentioned in the novel, which include scallops, sea clams, oysters, razor clams, and conch shells.

Sarah is also quite fond of flowers. We use the same kind of reference book to look up the flowers from the book. We try to see how many of the flowers we can find. If we can't find the actual flowers, then we try to find pictures of the flowers. See if your students can find examples of paintbrush, clover, prairie violets, roses, bride's bonnet, seaside goldenrod, wild asters, woolly ragwort, zinnias, marigolds, wild fever-few, dahlias, columbine, nasturtiums, and tansy.

■ Beyond Ideas

Family Portrait   Encourage students to draw portraits of the Witting family for the family's wedding album. They should use the descriptions in the book to draw the characters and the setting.

Next Chapter   Challenge students to write the next chapter in *Sarah, Plain and Tall*.

Comparison to the Movie   Hallmark Hall of Fame has made a movie out of the novel *Sarah, Plain and Tall*. Students love to watch the movie and then compare it to the book. They critique the director's choice of actors for the main roles and evaluate how true the actors were to the descriptions in the book. Students also compare the story line, setting, and so on. (I always love it when the students say they liked the book better than the film.)

■ Writing Idea

The Wittings really needed a wife and mother. Suggest that students think of something they really need and write ads for those things. Remind them that their ads should be clear and convincing, and should convey both the reason for their needs and the benefits of fulfilling them.

READING RESPONSE JOURNAL PROMPTS

Chapter 1: Why does Mr. Witting advertise for a wife?

Chapter 2: Why does Caleb read and reread Sarah's letters?

Chapter 3: Why does Anna wish that she, Papa, and Caleb were perfect for Sarah?

Chapter 4: Do you think Sarah will stay? Explain your reasons.

Chapter 5: Why do Caleb and Anna study Sarah's words so much?

Chapter 6: Why is Sarah asking about winter?

Chapter 7: How do you know Papa likes Sarah?

Chapter 8: a) Describe Sarah's character traits and use examples from the book to illustrate the traits.
b) Why does Sarah stay?

Dear Mr. Henshaw
by Beverly Cleary

1984 Newbery Medal

■ Summary

Dear Mr. Henshaw begins with Leigh Botts writing a letter to his favorite author, Mr. Henshaw, as a class assignment. The author writes back and asks Leigh some questions that his mother insists he answer. As Leigh answers Mr. Henshaw, we learn about his struggles with his parents' divorce, his relationship with his father, his loneliness because of being the new kid in town, and his feelings of being just medium. Mr. Henshaw encourages Leigh to keep a diary, and the book is written in that format.

■ Chapter by Chapter

Since there aren't any chapters in *Dear Mr. Henshaw*, do the cereal box project. You can find detailed explanation of this project on page 55 of this book (the **Chapter by Chapter** project for *The Whipping Boy*).

■ Into Ideas

Map of California   I give students outline maps of California and ask them to locate and label the following places: Bakersfield, Pacific Grove, Great Central Valley, and Highway 152—Pacheco Pass. I have them use their maps as we read the novel.

VOCABULARY

gondola	halyard
hibernated	imitate
insulated	nuisance
partition	snitch
wrath	

■ Through Ideas

Questions   Mr. Henshaw asks Leigh a series of probing questions on pages 14–30. I have students answer these questions about themselves. I also have them pretend that they are sending the answers to their favorite authors, so they take their time answering the questions.

Pictures of the Setting   The author gives a good description of the setting of this book (Leigh's neighborhood). Have students draw pictures of Leigh's neighborhood, including all the details the author gives (see pages 21–22).

Diary   Leigh learns to keep a diary in this novel. It helps him sort out his feelings and reflect on his life. Urge students to begin their own diaries and see what unfolds.

Lunch Box Alarm   Students are usually pretty excited about trying to make lunch box alarms of their own. Some

students are more adept at this kind of activity than other students are, so I give them the option of doing the assignment alone or with a friend or two. Then I have my young inventors bring their finished products to class so they can explain how they put the alarm together and demonstrate it. I find that a lot of parents get involved in this project.

■ Beyond Ideas

Meet the Authors   This is a perfect place to ask students to do a project on their favorite authors. I give talks on several different authors who have written a number of books, which helps spark students' interest. Some of the authors my students have enjoyed in the past include Avi, Lois Duncan, Lois Lowry, Joan Lowry Nixon, Scott O'Dell, Katherine Paterson, Gary Paulsen, Zilpha Keatly Snyder, Mildred Taylor, Theodore Taylor, Laurence Yep, and Jane Yolen.

Based on my talks, each student then makes an informed choice of an author. I group three or four students who have chosen the same author. Then I distribute to each group several books written by the author they selected. place students who have the same authors in mind in groups of three to four. The requirements are that each member of the group read at least one book by the author and that each group member pick a different book. I give students several weeks to read

their books; they usually read more books than I assign because they get involved in the books. I require students to make displays about their authors that will eventually hang in our local public library. The displays must be colorful, artistic, and accurate. They must prominently display the author's name and include the following elements:

- biography of the author
- list of other books written by the author
- summary and visual for each book read by the group (Summaries must be varied for each book. Students may choose to do their summaries in any of the following formats: letter, newspaper front page, diary entry, filmstrip or comic strip, interior monologue, or poem.)

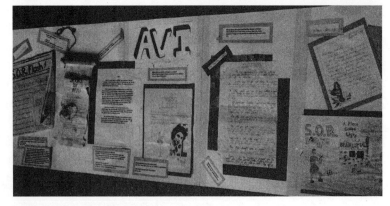

Students arrange all the required elements on three pieces of poster paper that have been taped together. We share the displays in class and then send them to the library for presentation. You can also ask your students to write letters to their authors, but be sure to do this ahead of time as it may take some time to receive answers. Students can include their letters and responses on their displays. I don't make this a requirement because some authors don't write back. Suggest that, to increase their chances of receiving an answer, students include self-addressed, stamped envelopes for the authors to use.

■ Writing Idea

Pose the following question to your students: *How did Leigh's parents divorce affect him?* Have them answer it using a five-paragraph essay format. Students should begin with an introduction that includes a thesis statement and three main points that will be explored in the essay. Paragraph two should be about the first main point in the introduction, along with details to support the point. Paragraph three should be about the second main point. Paragraph four about the third main point. Paragraph five is the conclusion.

READING RESPONSE JOURNAL PROMPTS

Pages 1-12: Why does Leigh's attitude toward Mr. Henshaw change?

Pages 14-30: Why does Leigh feel so medium?

Pages 31-37: Why does Mr. Henshaw keep answering Leigh's letters even though he is very busy?

Pages 38-44: Why does Leigh's mom refer to them as "lonely hearts"?

Pages 45-53: How does Mom feel about Leigh's Dad? How does Leigh feel about his dad?

Pages 55-59: Why is Leigh worried about his mom?

Pages 61-72: Why is Leigh mad at his father?

Pages 73-78: Why does Mom cry?

Pages 79-87: Why is Leigh angry at Dad?

Pages 89-104: How does Leigh's lunch box alarm change things for him?

Pages 105-111: Why does Leigh decide to start scrubbing the mildew off the bathroom?

Pages 112-121: Why does meeting Mrs. Badger make Leigh feel so good?

Pages 123-134: a) How can you explain Leigh's mixed feelings at the end of the book?
b) Why doesn't Beverly Cleary have Bonnie say she would like to get back together with Bill to make it a "happily ever after" ending?

Dicey's Song
by Cynthia Voigt

1983 Newbery Medal

■ Summary

The Tillerman children's mother is mentally ill and in the hospital. Dicey and her sister and brothers are adjusting to living with Gram—and she with them. Together, they struggle to become a true family. They also learn to reach out to others and not be afraid to love. Their mother never recovers, yet in the end her passing helps the family hold on to each other. *Dicey's Song* is the sequel to *Homecoming*.

■ Chapter by Chapter

Students enjoy doing the wheel book project for this novel. You can follow the instructions outlined on page 58 of this book (the **Chapter by Chapter** project for *Sarah, Plain and Tall*). Students will need to make the diameter of their circles bigger (12 inches is best) and divide the bottom circle into 12 equal parts for the 12 chapters in *Dicey's Song*

■ Into Ideas

Reading the Prequel   *Dicey's Song* is the sequel to Cynthia Voigt's *Homecoming*. For an Into activity, I like to read *Homecoming* aloud to my class. (I believe in reading aloud to my stu-

VOCABULARY

accusation	astound
aureole	chastened
civilization	deceitful
exasperated	extremes
fallow	harrumphed
indentured	intrusion
meandering	mercurochrome
minstrel	pert
plagiarism	precision
reminiscing	saunter
sedately	skeins
succulent	tendency
turgid	underpinnings
vaguely	

dents every day. I try to choose novels of different genres that will get them interested in different types of books for their free reading.) *Homecoming* is a wonderful book to read aloud, and it really helps my students have a better understanding when we read it as a core literature novel.

■ Through Ideas

Character Posters   There are many interesting characters in *Dicey's*

Song. I write the names on slips of paper and place them in a box. Then I have my students draw names out of the box. Depending on the size of my class that particular year, I sometimes have to put a character's name in the box more than once so that each student can draw a slip of paper. The characters I use are Dicey Tillerman, James Tillerman, Maybeth Tillerman, Sammy Tillerman, Gram, Millie Tydings, Mrs. Jackson, Miss Eversleigh, Mr. Chappelle, Wilhemina, Mr. Lingerie, and Jeff.

Students draw pictures of their characters on large sheets of construction paper. They can do a close-up or full shot or place the character in his/her setting. Students refer to the book to help them describe the physical characteristics of the characters, the roles the characters play in the novel, the characters' personalities, and then compare them to people in their own lives.

Joseph and the Many Colored Coat This Biblical story of Joseph and the Many Colored Coat is mentioned in the novel. It is important for students to know the story, so I read a version of it to my class. There are many collections of Bible stories for children, or you can always read aloud the story directly from the Old Testament of the Bible.

Fraction Lessons A great cross-curricular activity is to have students create lessons to help Maybeth understand the fractions 1/8 to 1/2. In the book, the family struggles with trying

to help Maybeth understand fractions, and it's fun and enlightening for students to try to come up with lessons themselves. If you are connected with a primary class, let your students try out their lessons on younger students. This really helps them get a feel for how difficult it is to teach these concepts and how to deal with the varying abilities of students in a classroom.

■ Beyond Ideas

Change the Ending Present the following situation to students:

Pretend that Momma does not die but comes home from the hospital to live with Gram and the children. How do you think this would affect the family? How do you think the story would end now? Write a description of how each character in the family would be affected, and write a new ending.

■ Writing Idea

Have your students write essays about their own families. Ask them to write about the people with whom they live and what role each person plays in their lives. And, finally, tell students to consider how they affect their own families.

65

READING RESPONSE JOURNAL PROMPTS

Chapter 1: What is your impression of Dicey?

Chapter 2: How does Dicey feel about the children becoming less dependent on her?

Chapter 3: Describe all the positives and negatives for Gram when the Tillerman children come to live with her.

Chapter 4: What does Dicey mean when she says the last sentence in this chapter?

Chapter 5: How is Dicey trying to hold on to her sister and brothers?

Chapter 6: Do you think James's plan to help Maybeth read will work? Explain why or why not.

Chapter 7: a) What would you do if you were Dicey when Mr. Chappelle accuses her of plagiarism?
b) Why does Gram make such a big deal about Dicey learning to reach out?

Chapter 8: How does reaching out change the family?

Chapter 9: a) Why has Dicey only thought about things a day ahead?

b) What does Mina mean when she says Dicey is "pretty strong meat"?
c) What is Dicey feeling as she looks at her Momma?

Chapter 10: Why does Gram send Dicey out to buy Christmas presents while she stays with Momma in the hospital?

Chapter 11: Why does Gram feel defeated?

Chapter 12: a) How is the Old Paper Mulberry tree like a family?
b) Why do you think Gram decides to bring out the albums?

The Westing Game
by Ellen Raskin

1979 Newbery Medal

■ Summary

The Westing Game brings 16 heirs together for the reading of Samuel W. Westing's will. The will turns out to involve a game to find out who murdered Westing. The story unfolds with plenty of twists and turns and has a fun cast of characters for students to follow and analyze. This is a great read in the mystery genre.

■ Chapter by Chapter

I have students use the story trail idea to follow the story in *The Westing Game*. The story trail idea is detailed on page 16 of this book (the **Chapter by Chapter** project for *The View From Saturday*).

■ Into Ideas

Introducing the Mystery Genre Most students have had experience with mystery books prior to reading *The Westing Game*. (I do, however, make sure that I have read aloud to them at least one mystery prior to this novel.) I ask stu-

VOCABULARY

adjacent	alibis
ample	appalled
bigot	calloused
cremated	culprit
derelicts	disguised
eccentric	facade
forfeited	immigrant
impeccable	incompetence
infirmity	inscrutable
lunatic	meager
meticulous	oblige
obsequious	paraphernalia
petrified	putrid
pyrotechnic	relinquishing
rigid	severe
tantrum	vindictive

dents if they have read Nancy Drew or Hardy Boys mysteries. Then we talk about more contemporary mysteries like *Wolf Rider* by Avi, *Don't Look Behind You* by Lois Duncan, *Following the Mystery Man* by Mary D. Hahn, *From the Mixed-Up Files of Mrs. Basil E. Frankweiler* by E.L. Konigsburg, and *Dew Drop Dead: A Sebastian Barth Mystery* by James Howe. We talk about the common elements of a mystery including the crime, suspects, and twists and turns in the plot that lead the reader to different conclusions. I also like to show my students a movie based on an Agatha Christie mystery; I stop it at several points to ask them to list what they know versus what they think. It's a lively start for students, and readies them for putting the pieces of the puzzle together and drawing conclusions when they start reading *The Westing Game*.

■ Through Ideas

Characters and Their Clues   There are 16 characters involved in the Westing game. I pair my students and assign a character to each set of partners. The partners make posters by drawing pictures of the characters and writing as many details about the characters as they can. These character posters are placed on the board. As we learn more about the characters, the partners add these details to their posters. This helps everyone keep track of the characters and the clues as they come up in the novel. The characters are Madame Sun Lin Hoo, James Shin Hoo, Doug Hoo, Grace Windsor Wexler, Jake Wexler, Turtle Wexler, Angela Wexler, Sydelle Pulaski, Alexander McSouthers, J.J. Ford, Berthe Erica Crow, Otis Amber, Christos Theodorakis, Theo Theodorakis, Flora Baumbach, and D. Denton Deere.

Paper Towel Clues   As the clues appear in the game, I have students write them on pieces of paper towel, as they were in the novel. Students see if they can try to put the mystery together before it actually gets solved in the book. I encourage my students to work cooperatively to see what they can conclude.

Whodunit?   Near the end of the book, the characters must reveal who they think did it based on the clues they have. At this point in the novel, I ask my students to write down who they think did it and why. I give each student an envelope in which to seal her or his answer. They write their names on the outside of the envelopes and return them to me. I keep the envelopes until we finish the novel, and then we open them to see how successful we were in solving the mystery.

■ Beyond Ideas

You're the Director   Urge students to pretend that they have been selected to direct the movie version of *The Westing Game*. They must cast 16 real-life actors and actresses to portray the main roles in the film. Remind them to choose the actor or actress for each role by staying true to the author's description of that character and his/her personality. Have students list their casting choices and the reasons for each choice.

■ Writing Idea

Here's your students' opportunity to be mystery writers. Have them write their own mysteries. Remind students that they will need to include a crime, suspects, clues, and clever ways to bring all the elements together. They can choose the reading of a will, or they may want to work backwards to write their mysteries by starting with the ending and working their way to the beginning.

READING RESPONSE JOURNAL PROMPTS

Chapter 1: Who do you think the wrong person is and why?

Chapter 2: Do you think the story of the bet is true?

Chapter 3: What do you think Sydelle Pulaski is up to?

Chapter 4: What do you think will happen at the reading of the will?

Chapter 5: How would you be feeling right now if you were sitting at the table waiting for the will to be read?

Chapter 6: How could all these people be related?

Chapter 7: Why do you think the partners are paired this way?

Chapter 8: Who steals the shorthand notes? Why do you think so?

Chapter 9: Do the findings of the newspaperman help you figure out who did it?

Chapter 10: How is the Westing game affecting the residents of Sunset Towers?

Chapter 11: Who shares their clues and why? Who won't share and why not?

Chapter 12: Why is Mr. Hoo happy about the exploding tomato sauce?

Chapter 13: How does the author keep your interest?

Chapter 14: What does the letter mean to you?

Chapter 15: Make two lists—one for the facts you've learned and the other for the gossip you've "heard" in this chapter.

Chapter 16: Who are your guesses for bomber, murderer, and thief? Justify your guesses.

Chapter 17: What is Crow talking about?

Chapter 18: Why do you think Dr. Deere is taking Chris to the hospital?

Chapter 19: What does Crow mean by two more days?

Chapter 20: Who do you think could be the ex-Mrs. Westing? Tell why.

Chapter 21: What do you think "purple mountain majesties" means? Why is Sydelle so excited about this?

Chapter 22: Why is Crow in real danger?

Chapter 23: Why do you think Sam Westing made the heirs play this game?

Chapter 24: Why does Berthe Erica Crow confess?

Chapter 25: Who is Sandy McSouthers?

Chapter 26: Who do you think is Westing's fourth identity? Explain your reasoning.

Chapter 27: Why does Westing continue to play games?

Chapter 28: What does each heir get out of playing the game?

Chapter 29: How have the heirs changed since their first meeting?

Chapter 30: Why is Turtle teaching her niece, Alice, to play chess?

Bridge to Terabithia
by Katherine Paterson

1978 Newbery Medal

■ Summary

Bridge to Terabithia is about a very special friendship between a boy and a girl. Jess and Leslie create an imaginary land, Terabithia, where they have wonderful adventures. Although the two friends come from different backgrounds, they learn much from each other. Then a terrible accident takes one of their lives and leaves the other to cope and carry on.

■ Chapter by Chapter

I ask my students to do a step book for *Bridge to Terabithia*. The step book allows them to illustrate and write summaries for each chapter, thereby looking at all the themes in this novel—friendship, family, revenge, peer pressure, and death. For a detailed description of what a step book is and how to put it together, see page 33 of this book (the **Chapter by Chapter** project for *The Giver*).

■ Into Ideas

Read Aloud *The Chronicles of Narnia* by C.S. Lewis is mentioned several times in this novel. A nice Into activity for this novel is to read one of the chronicles of Narnia to your students. This gives them an idea of what the characters are referring to in the novel and helps them with the fantasy, make-believe aspect of this work.

VOCABULARY

abruptly	accusation
anxiety	complacent
consolation	consolidated
conspicuous	cremated
dictators	exhilaration
exiled	faltered
hernia	humiliated
hypocritical	nuisance
ominously	pandemonium
repulsive	sacred
scorch	siege
speculation	sporadically
tyrants	upheaval
vigorously	

Create a Secret Kingdom Ask students to write descriptions of what perfect get-away, fantasy kingdoms would be for them. These should be make-believe places that they would love to escape to and have great adventures in.

■ Through Ideas

Illustrated Similes Katherine Paterson uses wonderful similes throughout her novel. This provides a great opportunity to show students how the use of similes can enhance their own writing.

I ask them to illustrate several of the similes that appear in the novel. I give each student a large construction-paper S and have him or her choose three similes from the novel. The students write and illustrate the similes on the S—one simile at the top, one in the middle, and one at the bottom. I start students off with the simile on page 19, "Surprise swooshed up from the class like steam from a released radiator cap." We talk about the visual image this creates and how much better and more descriptive it is than saying "The class was really surprised."

Dealing with Death   Have your students list and discuss all the things Jess does to deal with Leslie's death. Help them categorize these things to show the stages of healing—shock, denial, anger, guilt, remembering, and going on. Your students may come up with different names for the different stages; the most important thing is that they see there is a process.

Be prepared to have professional help for students who may have had something like this happen to them; the book may trigger strong memories and emotions. This year our school lost an eighth-grade boy in a terrible accident. I could not teach this book this year as the emotions were too raw. I know that teaching it in the next couple of years will continue to be very sensitive. Some students may not be ready to open up the wounds so soon.

■ Beyond Ideas

Quick Write   This quick-write is a five-to-seven-minute session of uninterrupted writing time. I ask students to quick write about what Jess means when he thinks, "Sometimes like the Barbie doll you need to give people something that's for them, not just something that makes you feel good giving it." After students share their quick write responses, I ask them to write about times when they may have applied this statement to their own lives. I also question them about what they think would happen if everyone in the world adopted this philosophy.

Dealing with Fear   Jess has a lot of fears. Discuss with students how his friendship with Leslie helps him face his fears. Make a list of their responses. Then talk about your students' own fears. Suggest that they make private lists of how they can deal with their fears.

■ Writing Idea

Present the following idea to your students:

Write a letter to a special friend. Tell that friend how he or she has changed your life. What do you appreciate about your friend? What are the qualities that make that person such a special friend? Mail the letter to your friend. How do you feel now? What do you think his or her reaction will be?

READING RESPONSE JOURNAL PROMPTS

Chapter 1: What are the Aarons family members like?

Chapter 2: Predict what will happen to Jess and Leslie.

Chapter 3: Why does Jess stand up for Leslie?

Chapter 4: a) Why does Jess decide to make it a new season in his life?
b) Why is Terabithia so important to Jess?

Chapter 5: Why does Jess feel bad about what they did to Janice Avery? Do you agree with what they did? Explain your decision.

Chapter 6: Compare Jess's Christmas with Leslie to his Christmas with his own family.

Chapter 7: Why is Jesse threatened by Leslie having one-and-a-half friends?

Chapter 8: How will Leslie answer the last question?

Chapter 9: Why does Jesse think it is better to be born without an arm than to go through life with no guts?

Chapter 10: How would you feel if you were Jesse right now?

Chapter 11: Why is Jesse acting so strangely?

Chapter 12: Why does Jesse say "I hate her"?

Chapter 13: How will Jess pass on all that he has learned from Leslie?

The Summer of the Swans

by Betsy Byars

1971 Newbery Medal

■ Summary

Sara is having a miserable summer. She questions her looks, her personality, and her family situation—and feels totally sorry for herself. When Charlie, her mentally retarded brother, gets lost, Sara realizes that the most important thing is to find him.

■ Chapter by Chapter

There are so many feelings and emotions for students to react to in *Summer of the Swans* that I ask them to keep double entry journals while reading it. I start the project by doing the first couple of chapters with the class. I use a large piece of chart paper to represent a journal and ask students to do the same thing with sheets of notebook paper. After writing Chapter 1 in the center of the top of the paper, I fold it half vertically to make two columns. At the top of the left column, I write *Notes, Facts*. At the top of the right column, I write *Quotes, Questions, Remarks*. Then I read chapter 1 with students and ask them to raise their hands when they come to an important item. I write all important items in the *Notes, Facts* side of the journal and have students do the same in their journals. As you continue to read aloud, model note-taking.

VOCABULARY

abruptly	accusation
agitation	anguish
cascade	chide
elongated	emphatically
indignation	inscrutable
kaleidoscope	pathetic
posse	revenge
spigot	wryly

Encourage students to react actively to the novel as you read. Write remarks and questions in the right column. After doing one or two chapters together, students are able to do the assignment independently. There are 23 chapters in *Summer of the Swans*, but I feel that it would be too tedious to do a double entry journal for every chapter. I ask students to choose 10 chapters to do. Because students choose different chapters, you are likely to have at least one sample for every chapter.

■ Into Ideas

Guest Speaker *Summer of the Swans* deals with the sensitive issue of mental

retardation. I want my students to handle this in a mature way. We are fortunate in that we have county classes for orthopedically and emotionally handicapped students. This is a great experience for my students to get to know these children as people and friends and not objects of jokes. I ask the teachers of our county classes to come in and speak to my class about their special-needs students. I ask them to talk about medical background as well as emotional needs. If you do not have classes like these on your campus, your county or district Office of Education will probably have a representative to send to your classroom.

■ Through Ideas

Character Cinquains I ask students to write cinquain poems for each of the main characters in the novel—Sara, Aunt Willie, Wanda, Charlie, Mary, and Joe Melby. The format for a cinquain is shown below.

> **Noun**
> **Adjective, adjective**
> **–ing verb, –ing verb, –ing verb**
> **Four-word free statement**
> **Synonym for the noun**

Students illustrate these poems if they wish, and I post them on our *Summer of the Swans* bulletin board. This way everyone can share their work and get a detailed look into the characters.

Communication Exercise To help students get an idea of the frustration Charlie and Sara feel in trying to communicate with each other, I have them try this exercise. I remind students that Charlie neither speaks nor writes and that he is slow to respond to Sara's questions. I pair students and give one partner a slip of paper that has a simple task on it like *I need water* or *I want my math book*. Without speaking or writing, students must try to get their partners to carry out the tasks. Students then trade roles so that each partner experiences the frustration. This is not a charades exercise—emphasize to students that they must place themselves in Charlie's shoes.

Steps Ask students to illustrate Sara's vision of the steps that appears on page 140 of the novel. Tell them to place Sara, her father, and Charlie on the appropriate steps. Then challenge students to place themselves on the steps. Where do they think they fit in? Have students explain their decisions.

■ Beyond Ideas

Self-Esteem Posters Sara questions herself throughout the novel. She places importance on her looks and what other people think of her. My students really relate to her feelings, and I think that is why they connect with this novel. To help students advertise their best personal qualities, I urge them to make posters about themselves. The posters should include the following:

- three different pieces of writing— an autobiography, a list of future

aspirations and dreams, and descriptions of either their families or friends

- two collages—one for dislikes and one for likes
- three photos—one recent, one as a young child, and one showing family

Students should put these items together in a colorful and creative display.

Classroom Buddies   As I mentioned earlier, we are fortunate enough to have county classes on our campus. To help students get to know our orthopedically and emotionally handi-capped students, I arrange a joint class where my students team with the county students to do an art project together. I work very closely with the county teacher so that this is a team approach. My students quickly find the limitations as well as the talents of their new friends.

■ Writing Idea

Sara makes the statement, "I think how you look is the most important thing in the world." Have students write essays that either agree or disagree with her statement.

READING RESPONSE JOURNAL PROMPTS

Chapter 1: Why does Sara feel it has been an awful summer?

Chapter 2: What kind of relationship does Sara have with Wanda? with Charlie?

Chapter 3: Why do Sara and Wanda have different views on Charlie?

Chapter 4: Why does Aunt Willie give in to Wanda regarding the motor scooter?

Chapter 5: Why does Sara think looks are the most important thing?

Chapter 6: How do you think Charlie feels when people talk about him?

Chapter 7: Why does Sara think she will never be content again?

Chapter 8: How does Wanda try to help Sara? Why doesn't it work?

Chapter 9: Predict what will happen to Charlie.

Chapter 10: Why is Charlie crying?

Chapter 11: How would you feel if you were Sara right now?

Chapter 12: Why does Aunt Willie caution Sara about revenge? Do you think she is right?

Chapter 13: Why does Sara think she has already lost her father?

Chapter 14: Why is Sara questioning the way she feels about Joe Melby?

Chapter 15: Why does Sara feel terrible once Mary tells her the true story of Charlie's missing watch?

Chapter 16: How does Sara feel about Joe now?

Chapter 17: Why does Charlie fall asleep?

Chapter 18: How is Sara feeling?

Chapter 19: Why doesn't Sara have any tears left to cry?

Chapter 20: How is Charlie trying to cope?

Chapter 21: Describe the feelings that Charlie, Sara, and Joe are experiencing right now.

Chapter 22: Why does Sara start to change the way she has felt about herself this summer?

Chapter 23: How do you know Sara has grown from this experience?

Sounder
by William H. Armstrong

1970 Newbery Medal

■ Summary

Sounder is the story of a great coon dog who is faithful to his master. Sounder's master is a sharecropper who has fallen on hard times. The sharecropper does what he must to provide food for his family. When men come to take away the sharecropper for stealing meat, Sounder is shot for trying to intervene. The sharecropper's son must take on the responsibilities of the household duties as his heart aches for his father and Sounder. The boy searches for his father and Sounder, and amidst all the injustices of the time, he is blessed for his faithfulness.

■ Chapter by Chapter

I begin the chapter by chapter assignment by talking to my students about the fact that the author never gives the characters names. They are called boy, mother, and father. We come to the conclusion that this was probably done to make this family and its story symbolic of the plight of many African American families during this time. I then talk to the students about symbols and ask them to do symbolic posters for *Sounder*. A detailed explanation of symbolic posters can be found on page 49 of this book (the **Chapter by Chapter** project for *Number the Stars*).

VOCABULARY

addled	animosity
calloused	carcass
cistern	compulsion
conjured	cruelty
eloquent	famished
gyrations	malicious
orneriness	poultice
rivulets	sowbelly

■ Into Ideas

Cover Impressions   I have students look at the cover of *Sounder*. I then ask them to write what they think the story is going to be about. Students save these impressions in their journals and compare what they wrote before reading the book to what they think after finishing it.

Introductory Quote   The following quote by Antoine de Saint-Exupéry appears on the opening page: "A man keeps, like his love, his courage dark." I ask students to tell me what they think the quote means. I have a class recorder keep track of the responses. We save the responses and look at them again after reading the novel to see if we have better insight into the quote.

■ Through Ideas

Visualizing the Author's Descriptions
I ask students to draw two pictures of Sounder using the author's descriptions. They must pay attention to all the details presented in the book. The first picture should be of Sounder in the beginning of the book and the second picture should be of Sounder after he is shot. I encourage students to include the setting around Sounder in both instances to be sure they really show the dramatic changes that took place.

Personification   Whenever I can, I like to show students the tools an author uses to bring the text to life. William H. Armstrong makes great use of personification in *Sounder*, and I ask students to find examples of personification throughout the novel. We keep a chart of the examples in the classroom. In the students' next writing assignment, I ask them to include at least one example of personification. Here is a good example from page 82 of *Sounder*: "The voice of the wind in the pines . . . . "

Metaphors   *Sounder* also provides good opportunities for students to look at metaphors in literature. I give them the quote from page 97, "'Some animal dug under the roots and tore them loose from the earth. It was wilted badly and might have died. But I reset it, and I water it every day. It's hard to reset a plant if it's wilted too much; the life has gone out of it. But this one will be all right. I see new leaves startin'.'" I ask students to use this quote as a metaphor for the boy's life. When students compare the boy's life to the plant's, they get a quick and clear picture of metaphor.

■ Beyond Ideas

Comparing the Book and the Movie
Cicely Tyson stars in a powerful film version of *Sounder*. I show the film to my students. Then I have them compare and contrast the film and the novel.

■ Writing Idea

Discrimination is a main theme in *Sounder*. Encourage students to write about times they or someone they know was discriminated against. Pose the following question to spur their thinking:

- *What happened?*
- *How did you feel?*
- *How can things be changed so that something like that won't happen again?*

READING RESPONSE JOURNAL PROMPTS

Chapter I: Why does the boy's mother keep humming?

Chapter II: Why don't the boy and his mother talk about what happened?

Chapter III: Why is the boy crying?

Chapter IV: a) Why does the boy's mother say that he must learn to lose?
b) Why is the boy so fearful?

c) How does the boy handle his anger? d) Why do the boy and his father have big quiet spells during their visit?

Chapter V: a) Why doesn't Sounder bark?
b) What happened to the boy's father?

Chapter VI: a) Why doesn't the boy remember how old he is?
b) How do you know the boy loves his father?

Chapter VII: a) Why doesn't the boy throw the iron at the white man?
b) Why does the boy trust the teacher?

Chapter VIII: a) Why does the mother say that the Lord has come to the boy?
b) Why does Sounder bark again for the first time in years?
c) What does the quote about the flower on page 116 mean to you?

A Wrinkle in Time
by Madeleine L'Engle

1963 Newbery Medal

■ Summary

This work of science fiction takes the reader on an adventure through a tesseract (a wrinkle in time) so that the Murry children can rescue their father from IT, the evil one. This is a story of the fight between good and evil set on other planets inhabited by wildly imaginative creatures. The overriding theme is that love can conquer all.

■ Chapter by Chapter

A step book works well with this novel. Students will need six sheets of paper to make twelve-step books. Detailed directions for making a step book appear on page 33 of this book (the **Chapter by Chapter** project for *The Giver*). Use one step for each of the twelve chapters in the novel.

A Wrinkle in Time
By Madeleine L'Engle

1 Mrs. Whatsit
2 Mrs. Who
3 Mrs. Which
4 The Black Thing
5 The Tesseract
6 The Happy Medium
7 The Man With Red Eyes
8 The Transparent Column
9 IT
10 Absolute Zero
11 Aunt Beast
12 The Foolish and the Weak

VOCABULARY

accuracy	agility
antagonistic	assimilate
belligerent	bilious
corporeal	dais
delinquent	despondency
deviate	dilapidated
ephemeral	exclusive
fallible	frenzy
indignant	judiciously
myopic	pedantic
peremptory	physicist
prodigious	relinquish
sarcastic	serenely
subdue	supine
tractable	trepidation
vulnerable	

■ Into Ideas

Story Impression Using Chapter Titles   *A Wrinkle in Time* has wonderful chapter titles. I use this to my advantage by having students write story impressions based on the chapter titles. I write the chapter titles on the board as follows:

Mrs. Whatsit

Mrs. Who
Mrs. Which
The Black Thing
The Tesseract
The Happy Medium
The Man With Red Eyes
The Transparent Column
IT
Absolute Zero
Aunt Beast
The Foolish and the Weak

Students make up stories that include all of these chapter titles. They have a great time coming up with imaginative stories, and this process helps them to connect to the novel because they continually check their stories against the author's as we read.

■ Through Ideas

Character Webs   To help students keep track of the characters and their characteristics and roles in the novel, I have students do character webs. The title goes in the center of the web and branching out from it are the name of the characters. They add each character as he or she, or it, appears in the novel, along with characteristics and the role the character has in the novel.

Picture of the Setting   The book contains a very detailed description of the Murry home, and specifically the kitchen, that offers an opportunity for students to practice visualizing settings. I ask them to draw pictures of one setting inside the house, being careful to include every element about

which the author has written.

Picture of a Difficult Character
When Mrs. Whatsit undergoes a metamorphosis, it may be difficult for students to visualize the character change without rereading the passage. I find my students just want to keep reading and gloss over things that are difficult at first. So I ask them to draw pictures of the changed Mrs. Whatsit so that they will have to reread to get a true vision of her metamorphosis.

Research Reports   A good interdisciplinary activity for students to do is to write research reports on the famous personalities from history that are alluded to in *A Wrinkle in Time*. These include Jesus, Leonardo da Vinci, Shakespeare, Pasteur, Einstein, Gandhi, Beethoven, St. Francis, Copernicus, Bach, Michelangelo, Madame Curie, Albert Schweitzer, Buddha, Rembrandt, and Euclid.

■ Beyond Ideas

Complete the Trilogy   *A Wrinkle in Time* is part of a trilogy. The other two titles are *A Wind in the Door* and *A Swiftly Tilting Planet.* My students are always eager to read the other two books written by Madeleine L'Engle. I usually read one of the books aloud and have several copies on hand of the third book for students to explore on their own.

Sonnets   The power of love is an overriding theme in this novel, so I ask my

students to write sonnets to tell about *A Wrinkle in Time*. A sonnet is a poem with fourteen lines of verse. Each verse is written in iambic pentameter (five metrical feet with each foot having one short syllable followed by one long syllable, or one unstressed syllable followed by one stressed syllable). I provide examples of sonnets for students to study.

■ Writing Idea

Present the following situation to your students:

If you could travel through a tesseract, a wrinkle in time, to either the past or the future, which would you choose and why? Be specific about the time period and place you choose. Why are you drawn to that place and time? What would you expect or hope

READING RESPONSE JOURNAL PROMPTS

Chapter 1: How does Mrs. Whatsit affect Charles? Meg? Mrs. Murry?

Chapter 2: Why does Charles know so much?

Chapter 3: Why does Meg wish she were a different person?

Chapter 4: Why does the dark thing seem evil?

Chapter 5: How do you think the group is going to fight evil?

Chapter 6: What do you think is going on in the town?

Chapter 7: What has happened to Charles?

Chapter 8: Do you agree with Camazotz's theory that differences create problems? Explain why or why not.

Chapter 9: How does IT control people?

Chapter 10: Predict what will happen next.

Chapter 11: Explain sight to Aunt Beast.

Chapter 12: Why is love the only thing that IT could not control?

1959 Newbery Medal

The Witch of Blackbird Pond
by Elizabeth George Speare

■ Summary

The Witch of Blackbird Pond takes place during 1687–1688. After the death of her grandfather, with whom she has been living in luxury, Kit Tyler leaves Barbados to find her only living relatives in America. Saddened by the death of her grandfather but hopeful that her aunt and uncle will welcome her, Kit sets sail on the brigantine *Dolphin* for the Connecticut Colony. She doesn't find a welcoming home when she arrives; her aunt and uncle are Puritans, and life is very hard and different for her. When Kit befriends a lonely woman who has been cast out of the community as a witch, she is accused of being a witch herself. Through it all, Kit gains the love and trust of her family and finds a love of her own.

VOCABULARY

adroit	allegiance
auspiciously	brandishing
brigantine	condescension
deliberation	diligently
heathen	hypocrite
ingenious	insubordination
malicious	menial
nonchalance	obstreperous
poignant	pompous
premonition	punctilious
raiment	sepulcher
staid	timorous
tremulous	vengeance

■ Chapter by Chapter

A fun idea for a chapter by chapter project is to have your students make a chapter quilt. The directions for making the quilt are on page 6 of this book (the **Chapter by Chapter** project for *Out of the Dust*).

■ Into Ideas

Read a Play   This novel concerns the witch scare of the 1600's. Belief in the powers of evil was strong during this time; strict and demanding religious practices were adhered to, especially by the Puritans. Those who were different, who had strange markings on their bodies or who talked to themselves, were often accused of being witches—and it was very difficult to prove you weren't a witch. I found a wonderful play that I like to have my students read before we get into *The Witch of Blackbird Pond*. It gives them some insight into the paranoia of the times, and they love reading plays. The play is called "On Trial in Salem" and can be

found in READ Magazine, Vol. 41, No. 6, November 15, 1991.

Map Work   Duplicate outline maps of North America for students. Have them prepare maps of colonial America with the following locations: Barbados; the West Indies; Antigua; Connecticut, including Wethersfield, Saybrook, New London, and Hartford; Massachusetts, including Boston; Louisiana, including New Orleans; the Caribbean Sea; the Atlantic Ocean; and the Connecticut River.

■ Through Ideas

Jigsawing Information   There are many topics in the book with which students may not be familiar. I ask them to jigsaw these topics. A detailed explanation of how to set up a jigsaw appears on page 52 of this book (the **Into Ideas** activity for *Hatchet*). The topics I use include New England colonial villages, Puritans, Quakers, punishment in New England (pillory, whipping posts, stocks), blue laws, the Salem witch trials, and King Charles.

Nat Chart   Nat does many things that should lead the reader to realize his feelings for Kit. Ask your students to make charts of all the things that Nat does that prove he cares for Kit. You can also have them record the personal qualities of Nat, John Holbrook, and William Ashby. Who do they think is best for Kit and why?

Matthew Wood   Matthew Wood changes a lot from the beginning of the novel to the end. I ask students to record the changes in him as we read. They place the changes on the left-hand side of their papers, and on the right-hand side, they write why they think Matthew underwent each change.

Dramatize the Trial   Students love acting out the part of the novel where Kit is tried. I place them in two groups so that everyone has plenty of acting time and involvement with the script. Students write their own scripts based on the novel and act out the scenes.

■ Beyond Ideas

Letter to Hannah   Have students pretend they are Kit and write letters to Hannah. They should let Hannah know how much she is missed and what has happened to Kit since she left.

■ Writing Idea

Kit doesn't fit in in her new home and

community. Have your students ever felt that they didn't fit in? Ask them write about their experiences. Encourage students by asking questions like the following:

- *How did this change affect your life?*
- *How did you feel?*
- *How has the experience changed you?*

READING RESPONSE JOURNAL PROMPTS

Chapter 1: Why do Nat and John Holbrook warn Kit?

Chapter 2: Why does Kit feel so unwelcome in Wethersfield?

Chapter 3: How would you feel about your new home if you were Kit?

Chapter 4: Compare Kit's life in Barbados to her cousins' lives in Wethersfield.

Chapter 5: Why does Kit regret coming to Wethersfield?

Chapter 6: Why is Matthew Wood so offended by Rev. Bulkeley?

Chapter 7: Why does William Ashby appeal to Kit even though they have little in common?

Chapter 8: Why is Matthew Wood so hard and contrary?

Chapter 9: How does Hannah help Kit?

Chapter 10: Why does the town think Hannah is a witch?

Chapter 11: Why does Kit take risks with Prudence? with Hannah?

Chapter 12: Do you think Kit will obey her Uncle's orders? Tell why or why not.

Chapter 13: What do you think John Holbrook will do?

Chapter 14: Why is Kit going to wait until the **Dolphin** is well on its way to Saybrook before she delivers the package to Hannah?

Chapter 15: Why is Kit proud of Uncle Matthew?

Chapter 16: Why does John Holbrook enlist in the militia?

Chapter 17: Why are the townspeople after Hannah?

Chapter 18: What will happen to Kit?

Chapter 19: Why do Prudence and Nat risk everything to help Kit?

Chapter 20: What is Kit's dream? Why is it necessary?

Chapter 21: Why are Kit and Nat a good match?

The Cat Who Went to Heaven

by Elizabeth Coatsworth

 1931 Newbery Medal

■ Summary

The Cat Who Went To Heaven is a charming Japanese fable that gives many details of Buddha's life. A poor, young artist is commissioned to do a painting of the death of Buddha for the temple. To make his painting come to life, the artist imagines scenes from Buddha's life. While the artist works, his faithful cat Good Fortune watches. As a tribute to Good Fortune, the artist includes the cat in his painting. The temple priests are outraged because the cat rebelled against Buddha and therefore did not receive his blessing. They order that the painting be burned. By a miracle, the painting is saved, a valuable lesson is learned, and the young artist is rewarded. This is a great book to use with the study of ancient religions and civilizations.

■ Chapter by Chapter

Since this book does not have any chapters, I ask my students to make book maps of the story as they go along. The book map begins with an outline picture of something symbolic in the book drawn in the center of the page; for example, a cat would be an excellent choice in this case. Written within the picture is the title of the book. Branching out from the picture

VOCABULARY

apparition	besieged
betrayer	brandishing
contemplation	dexterity
dignity	hydrangeas
lacquer	narcissus
palanquin	sagacity

are the following topics: setting, characters, events, conflict/problems, resolutions, and themes. The students write in the appropriate information for each topic.

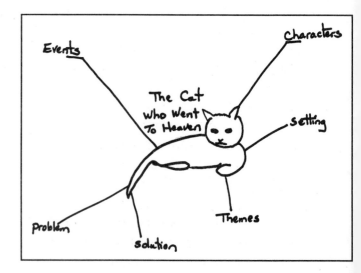

■ Into Ideas

Student Topics   Some of your students may be of Japanese descent or know a lot about Japanese culture. I ask for student volunteers who have expertise in any of the following areas to sign up to give mini-talks, and I give them extra credit. The topics I assign are Siddhartha, the tea ceremony, foods (rice cakes, dumplings, sweet bean jelly), Japanese painting, Buddha, and any other customs that students might want to share from the Japanese culture. If you don't have any students who can deliver these mini-talks, then reach out to your community for guest speakers.

■ Through Ideas

Storytelling   Break *The Cat Who Went To Heaven* into parts, and assign the parts to groups of students. The groups then retell their parts of the story as they show original illustrations they have drawn.

Animal Lessons   Assign to students the animals highlighted in the story. Have each student memorize the story that goes with the animal, draw an illustration for it, and then share what he or she thinks the lesson of that story is. The following animals have stories in the novel: Swan, Buffalo, Snail, Elephant, Horse, Dog, Deer, Ape/Monkey, and Tiger.

Songs of the Housekeeper   There are eight songs of the Housekeeper in the novel. I divide my class into eight groups of four students each and assign at random one song to each group. Each group must decide how to present the song to the class. They can pick any format they want, but they must also illustrate the song. This way we can display the illustrations around the room as the story unfolds. The groups must also discuss with the class the significance of the songs.

■ Beyond Ideas

Other Religions   This novel deals with Buddha's ideal of being able to love and forgive one another. Ask students to investigate to see if the ideal of loving and forgiving one another is found in other religions. (This is an especially good activity for sixth-grade students in California as the state framework requires the history of many religions to be taught at that grade.)

Draw Your Final Impression   We are never shown the artist's final painting, but it is described very well. Ask your students to draw their impressions of what the final painting looks like based on the author's description. Hang the final products on your bulletin board, and compare the details. If your students are nervous about their artistic abilities, you can always pair students for this activity. Have one student guide the artist by checking the facts in the novel and giving direction.

■ Writing Idea

Ask students to ch̲... ...ate the morals. You may want to
they think is important such as "Do ...nstorm ...th students to get them
unto others as you would have them do ...stance, if students are
unto you," and write stories to illus- stuck, ask them to think of some
things that happen in their everyday
lives that would support their morals.

READING RESPONSE JOURNAL PROMPTS

Pages 1-12: a) Why does the housekeeper get a cat instead of food?
b) Why do you think the author picked Good Fortune for its name?

Pages 13-19: Why does the artist laugh like a boy again?

Pages 22-31: Why does the artist try to make Siddhartha's life come alive in his thoughts?

Pages 33-41: How does the artist make sure his paintings of the animals are just right?

Pages 43-52: Why does Good Fortune leave?

Pages 56-60: Why does Good Fortune get sadder with each painting?

Pages 61-68: Why does Good Fortune die?

Pages 70-73: Why is the painting changed? What message does it send?